T0248260

The
Deaf
Girl

The Deaf Girl

A Memoir of Hearing Loss, Hope, and Fighting Against the Odds

ABIGAIL HERINGER

Copyright © 2024 by Abigail Heringer
Cover and internal design © 2024 by Sourcebooks
Cover design by Sarah Brody/Sourcebooks
Cover image © Spencer Click
Back cover image © Josh Erb
Internal design by Laura Boren/Sourcebooks

This publication is designed to provide accurate and authoritative information in regard to the subject matter covered. It is sold with the understanding that the publisher is not engaged in rendering legal, accounting, or other professional service. If legal advice or other expert assistance is required, the services of a competent professional person should be sought.—*From a Declaration of Principles Jointly Adopted by a Committee of the American Bar Association and a Committee of Publishers and Associations*

This book is not intended as a substitute for medical advice from a qualified physician. The intent of this book is to provide accurate general information in regard to the subject matter covered. If medical advice or other expert help is needed, the services of an appropriate medical professional should be sought.

This book is a memoir. It reflects the author's present recollections of experiences over a period of time. Some names and characteristics have been changed, some events have been compressed, and some dialogue has been re-created.

Published by Sourcebooks
P.O. Box 4410, Naperville, Illinois 60567–4410
(630) 961-3900
sourcebooks.com

Cataloging-in-Publication Data is on file with the Library of Congress.

Printed and bound in the United States of America.
VP 10 9 8 7 6 5 4 3 2 1

This book is dedicated to my mother, Suzie,
who taught us that we all have a place in this world.
Your unconditional love, support and encouragement
has been my biggest blessing in my life.
We are deeply grateful for every sacrifice
you've made for our family.
I love you.

Introduction

I sat in the limousine, surrounded by chatter I couldn't quite hear, staring at women that were supermodel gorgeous. If they were nervous, they didn't show it. When the limousine attendant offered everyone a glass of champagne, I was the only one who took him up on the offer. It probably wasn't true, but at the time, it seemed like I was the only one who needed some liquid courage to calm the nerves.

The more the other women talked among themselves, the less I was able to hear. Unable to join in the conversation, I focused instead on repeating in my head the line that I'd say when I met Matt on the steps of Nemacolin.

What on earth was I doing here? This wasn't something I'd ever imagined for myself. I'd been a longtime fan of *The Bachelor*, but I never actually pictured myself on the show. I applied mostly as a joke. Covid had taken over the world, I was laid off from my job, and I found the application for the show while I was searching for employment ads. But when I got the call that they wanted me on the show, I knew I couldn't say no.

Not just because Matt was a very handsome, seemingly down-to-earth guy (though he was, and I was so excited to get a chance to meet him). There was more to it than that. Because there was something about me that was different from every other woman in the limo. Different from every woman who had ever been on *The Bachelor*, actually.

I repeated my line in my head once more. "I'm going to be reading your lips a lot tonight, because I'm deaf. But thankfully, you've got beautiful lips, so I can't complain."

I was the first deaf contestant on *The Bachelor*. That's why I couldn't pass up this opportunity.

When I called to tell my mom, who is usually very private and reserved, about my invitation to go on *The Bachelor*, I thought she'd shut it down right away. We'd watched the show together, so she knew how crazy it could get. I figured she wouldn't want me in the limelight like that. But what she said surprised me.

"I think that's great. You could teach a lot of people about cochlear implants."

How often did an opportunity like this come knocking? When was another woman with a cochlear implant going to be invited to the show? It could be years; it could be never.

I'd never seen someone like me on reality TV. So as hopeful as I was about meeting Matt, I knew I could do something good here.

So here I was—the quiet girl who didn't like attention—going on an international television show. Not only that, but from the very start, I was going to have to step out of this limo and be forthcoming about my disability. Even in my normal dating life, that wasn't something I'd mastered, choosing often to wait until a third or fourth date to talk about my cochlear implant.

I'd spent most of my life trying to blend in with the able-bodied crowd around me, never wanting to stand out as the "deaf girl." For so many years, I was two people—the Abigail who was deaf and the Abigail who was just me.

But both versions of Abigail were always quiet, always unassuming, always blending into the background. So who was this person who decided she was going to speak about her disability in the most public forum possible?

I was about to find out, and fast. The limousine was pulling up, all the women were waving, me included. I was the closest to the door, the first one in our vehicle who had to step out into the night to meet Matt.

I was so viscerally aware that I wasn't just meeting Matt; I was meeting the entire world. I wasn't just speaking to him but speaking to *everyone* about my disability and experience with cochlear implants.

But here's the thing, I have never been one to speak up. Finding my voice had been a journey up until this point. I thought I'd done it, thought that at the age of twenty-five, I'd worked out the little kinks of figuring out who I was and how to approach the world confidently as a disabled woman. *The Bachelor* was about to be a new journey, though. One that would challenge me in ways I couldn't even imagine and bring me into the life I have today. But to understand that journey, I first have to bring you on another one. The one that led me to be the woman who agreed to go on *The Bachelor*. And that journey, surprisingly, doesn't actually begin with me.

It begins with my sister.

Chapter 1

For most people, their life story begins the day they were born. That is when their legacy starts. But not mine. My life story precedes my birth. It's my sister Rachel who started my legacy. While I was still in my mother's womb, she introduced my family to the same medical condition that would invariably impact the rest of my life. There is no way for me to tell my story without first telling hers.

For the first twelve months of her life, Rachel appeared to be a perfectly healthy baby. My mom, Suzie, had her plan for motherhood well mapped out. She'd read all the baby books, including the classic *What to Expect When You're Expecting*, and had weekly Mommy and Me classes with Rachel where she connected with other first-time parents. Having a new baby is always stressful to some degree, but with my mother's type A personality, she was well prepared. It's crazy to think that she was younger than I am now as I write out the story of our lives, and yet parenting came so naturally for her. She was prepared in a way I'm not sure I would be. And that preparation had paid off. The first year of Rachel's life had gone really well. She was hitting all her milestones right on time.

Until she wasn't.

Mom was incredibly close to my grandparents, who lived only five minutes away. In my younger years, it was so natural for me to see my grandparents nearly every day. They were an integral part of our lives, though I wouldn't know just how special that bond was until I was much older. While I'm pretty sure they would've been close to us regardless, what Mom was about to learn definitely pulled everyone closer together.

Grandpa retired the same year Rachel was born, and my granny had been a stay-at-home mom, so the both of them were always available to spend time with Rachel. Going to their house was a reprieve for Mom. It served as a place where she could relax and unwind while my grandparents doted on little Rachel.

On the day of Rachel's twelve-month pediatrician visit, Mom dropped by to have a cup of coffee before heading to the doctor's office. She sat Rachel in her high chair with some crackers, and Granny grabbed a Dr. Seuss book to read.

"'I do not like green eggs and ham. I do not like them, Sam-I-am,'" she'd say in the heavy Scottish accent that I remember so fondly.

But I wasn't born with the ability to hear that accent, and neither was Rachel. Granny didn't notice that Rachel wasn't responding to *Green Eggs and Ham*. Babies aren't exactly known for their extended eye contact, so it was hard to tell.

Rachel loved seeing Granny though, and her excitement was the only thing Mom took note of as she sipped her cup of coffee at the round oak table that still had crayon markings from Rachel's previous visit. Based on my own experiences, I know that Rachel was feeding off Granny's infectious positive energy. It's funny, all I remember of my childhood is positive memories, despite all the scary audiologist appointments and surgeries that came my way. I don't remember being afraid before my cochlear implant surgery, I only remember having cake in my hotel room the night prior. It's mostly through writing this book with information from Mom that I'm learning of my own childhood struggles. Just goes to show how much children feed off the energy that the adults in their life provide them, and my mom and grandparents were a source of peace for me. Similarly, for Rachel, there was a peace that coated that afternoon, the calm before the storm.

On the way out, Mom went to say goodbye to Grandpa, who was reading a newspaper on the living room couch. "Alright, we're off to see Dr. Buzz."

He paused, looking from Rachel to my mom. "When you see Dr. Buzz, ask him to check Rachel's hearing." He almost squinted at Rachel as he said the words.

From Mom's perspective, this was nothing more than an offhand comment, but it would soon change the trajectory of Rachel's life. To this day, my mom still isn't sure what caused my grandpa to suggest this. He was a general surgeon and commented on these types of things often, so she didn't even think to question him. It all just seemed commonplace at the time.

In retrospect, there were some signs that Rachel might be deaf, but they were easy to miss as a first-time mother. Rachel hadn't spoken her first word yet by twelve months, and Mom was aware of this, but it didn't worry her because Rachel had an extensive repertoire of babbling noises, a sign that she would start speaking soon.

Except they weren't *really* babbling noises. Not having another baby to compare her behavior to, it was easy for Mom to mistake the guttural noises that Rachel made for babbling. But her noises were not mimicking the tones she heard the adults around her make. They were noises that Rachel could *feel*, that caused a rumbling in her throat and body. Even as someone who once made those same noises, I'm not even sure I could tell the difference between a baby copying the sounds they hear and a baby using noise to cause vibrations in their body. Because Rachel was making noises, Mom assumed she must be hearing fine.

At first, the appointment seemed to go off without a hitch. Nurse Dottie checked Rachel's height and weight, which were in the normal range. In the small exam room, Rachel sat in Mom's lap, happy as could be. Mom almost forgot entirely about what Grandpa had said.

"Everything looks great," Nurse Dottie comfortingly smiled down at Rachel. "Do you have any questions or concerns before I grab the doctor?"

Mom looked at Rachel, who once again started making little grunting noises. That's when Grandpa's words echoed in her mind.

"My dad did tell me to ask about her hearing." The words came out nonchalantly because that's how Mom felt.

But Nurse Dottie did not share Mom's casual attitude. She straightened up, her demeanor shifting ever so slightly. "Well, that's a very serious concern. I'll definitely speak to the doctor about it."

Dr. Buzz gave a referral to an audiologist straight away, which my mom saw as merely a precautionary measure rather than a sign something was wrong. Dr. Buzz didn't do any of the testing himself. While some pediatricians will administer rudimentary hearing tests by snapping their fingers near a baby and gauging their reaction, Dr. Buzz was wary of the often-inaccurate results. A baby could use their other senses to assess what was happening around them. Rachel might feel the small rush of air that came with a snap, or witness a hand moving in her peripheral vision, and those reactions would not be indicative of whether she could hear. A visit with the audiologist would give much clearer results.

Mom left with Rachel and continued with the rest of their day as planned. When my biological father came home, she told him about the referral, but he didn't see a reason to worry either. The appointment would happen during his work hours, so Mom didn't even ask him to go, fully expecting to find that Rachel was fine. Personally, I'm a bit of a worrier, someone who is often imagining the worst-case scenario for any given situation. But even I wouldn't have imagined a deaf diagnosis if I was in my mom's shoes. I mean, Rachel was a healthy, responsive newborn. It's human nature for our minds to resist such a dramatic shift in what we know to be true, and what my parents knew to be true was that Rachel was a happy baby.

Finding out anything else would have shifted the state of their entire world. I don't think anyone is ever capable of imagining their life turning upside down, but it was especially difficult for my mom, who had such a clear-cut plan for motherhood.

That plan had to change significantly after Rachel's audiology appointment. They were brought back to a closet-size room with a door so heavy my mom could feel the airtight seal when it closed. I would later come to know these testing rooms well, so I can say with confidence that these rooms would be a nightmare for anyone with claustrophobia. They're a somber space, with absolutely no outside noise or white noise. For me, they're a comfort, because true silence is my natural state of being and something I crave if I've had my cochlear implant on too long. But for my mom, and anyone else who is used to hearing sound, they can be disconcerting. I'm sure it was especially bothersome for Mom because she didn't know yet that Rachel would've been comfortable in this closed-in echo chamber.

A small window allowed the test administrator to look in from the hallway and assess Rachel's reactions. On the left and right side of the room, behind glass, sat a toy monkey. Any time a noise was played, the toy would move, so the kids had an item to seek out as the source of any sound.

Besides the monkey, only a few toys sat in front of an empty chair. Too many toys could have distracted Rachel from the task at hand. My mom took her seat, setting Rachel down on the floor by her feet.

Rachel didn't have much of a reaction. She was comfortable in the quiet, unaware that she should be reacting at all. As the noises echoed from the left and right at various volumes, Rachel continued to fiddle with the wooden blocks in front of her. It was a red flag, but Mom didn't know that yet. She still expected that when they walked out of that small room, she'd learn Rachel had perfect hearing. I don't think she was in denial as much as she had just never even imagined a world where Rachel couldn't hear.

Mom walked out of the testing room with short-lived confidence.

"I am so sorry," the audiologist said gently after the sound-proof door closed behind them. "Rachel didn't pass her screening."

"What?" Mom's heart sank as her mind struggled to process this, her entire body denying what it had just heard.

But the sympathy in the audiologist's voice could not be mis-understood. This was not good news.

"Rachel didn't hear any of those noises. A hearing child

would've been startled by some of the sounds. Typically, they'd be turning their head to look for a person or musical toy to find the source of the noise."

Though my mom hadn't considered this in the booth, it made perfect sense. Rachel hadn't turned her head once.

In an instant, the concrete plans Mom had made for Rachel's life were cracking. Would the steady future she had hoped for her daughter still be possible? So many variables had suddenly come into play.

With hearing loss, it isn't just the ability to hear that a person loses; it's their ability to speak and understand those around them. If Rachel couldn't hear, she wouldn't be able to talk to anyone. How would she make friends? Or attend school? This could mean Rachel would have to rely on American Sign Language (ASL), and her choices of school and friendships would be limited to the Deaf community—which wasn't necessarily a bad thing, but it was a shock to my mom, whose community consisted of only hearing people. Would Rachel ever belong to the community that my mom had built? There are so many small intricacies of hearing loss that have a far-reaching impact on a developing baby.

It was a tangled web Mom had to unravel bit by bit. She thought she'd already done a lot of research on child development, but no baby book could prepare her for this. Mom didn't even know another deaf person. And this was before the internet. Knowledge wasn't a simple click away.

The barrier of the unknown was a twelve-foot wall standing

between my mom and Rachel's future. There was no easy ladder to get her over it, only a long steady climb. How was she going to help Rachel when she didn't even fully understand her condition?

As hard as hearing the news was, sharing it with others was even worse. My mom went straight from the audiologist to my grandparents' house.

When she walked in, she wasn't crying, and she hadn't cried at the audiologist's office either. She was in a state of shock, processing internally but not outwardly. This is something Mom and I have always had in common. I've never been a big crier, preferring not to wear my emotions on my sleeve.

So when she told me she had burst into tears after telling my grandparents that Rachel failed her screening, I knew how hard this must have been for her. I can probably count on one hand how many times I've seen my mom cry. But telling Granny and Grandpa made the news real, and that reality was hard to cope with.

Granny was equally stoic in nature, but she hugged my mom, suppressing her own tears.

As hard as this news was for Mom, it was compounded for my grandparents. In addition to their concern for Rachel, they had to watch their own child struggle with the news while they could do nothing to lift the burden. My grandfather, having worked in the medical field, had a greater understanding than my mom did of how significantly this would impact Rachel's development.

When my mother would later share the news with friends, it was a bit easier because they didn't fully understand the extent of what hearing loss could mean for Rachel's life. At that age, Rachel was still an adorable baby whom they could all hold and cuddle. The future that Rachel might live in was a distant one. But my grandparents were acutely aware of how difficult hearing loss could be and how it would shape Rachel as she developed.

"Don't worry, Suzie. We're going to figure this out," Granny told her.

And she meant it. If there is one thing my family doesn't do, it's dwell. There was no sitting around to grieve. Everyone was focused on action. What was the next step they needed to take? What could they do for Rachel right now?

That's part of what made the diagnosis so difficult. Nobody really knew. More tests needed to be run, and my mom was referred to the Eugene Hearing and Speech Center. But answers were few and far between, leaving my mom with the heavy weight of uncertainty.

It wasn't the fact that Rachel would have a disability that bothered Mom. She'd always been a firm believer that everyone had a place in the world. She just hated not knowing what Rachel's future was going to look like.

One night, Mom was trying to balance her stress while laying Rachel down in her crib. Rachel was fussing, and Mom spun a rainbow mobile dotted with small cartoon animals in hopes it would calm her down. Then it hit her: Rachel couldn't even hear the mobile.

The gravity of it all pulled her down. She stared at Rachel, who was settling into her crib mattress in a navy onesie, and Mom allowed herself to fully grasp the reality of the situation for the first time.

Her poor baby. How hard was life going to be for her? What would her world look like now that she couldn't hear? The mobile couldn't calm her, and all this time, Mom assumed Rachel could hear it. Really, Mom knew nothing about Rachel's experiences for her first year of life. She perceived the world in a completely different way than Mom had thought.

Still, Rachel stared up, and her eyes followed the colorful wheel above her. And that's when the *real* truth hit my mom.

Rachel's world hadn't actually changed at all. Mom may have just learned about the hearing loss, but the hearing loss hadn't occurred in an instant. Rachel was born this way. She'd never been able to hear. The mobile had always been silent to her, and yet, it had always calmed Rachel down.

All those happy moments at Mommy and Me classes, where Rachel smiled as she observed her environment, those had happened without Rachel ever being able to hear. Rachel had always been a joyful baby. Being deaf hadn't impacted that. My mom's life was suddenly thrust into disarray, so it was easy to believe that Rachel's life had been too. But the only thing that had changed was my mother's perception of Rachel's world. For Rachel, nothing had changed, and she was happy as ever.

So if Rachel was happy and well-adjusted, then the only thing Mom had to change was her perception. And she did. Rachel was happy, and Rachel could not hear. Those two truths could exist in the same universe. All Mom could do was learn and get Rachel the help she needed to continue developing.

There was still a lot to learn about Rachel's condition, but Mom was no stranger to research. She had a master's degree in counseling and a passion for learning. Mom absorbed and utilized every resource given to her, which included an appointment at the Eugene Hearing and Speech Center.

Things were moving fast, though never quite fast enough for Mom. There wasn't a minute of her day when she wasn't thinking about Rachel's condition. But she did her best to try and relax when possible.

TV was the easiest way to do that. If Mom was fully absorbed in a show, her brain would be too preoccupied to stress about Rachel. One night she was folding laundry in front of the TV and flipped through the channels, ultimately settling on the Miss America pageant. It seemed as good a distraction as any from the chaos that had become her world. But when contestant Heather Whitestone showed up on screen, Mom realized this wasn't going to be a distraction from Rachel's condition. Instead, the pageant would serve as an opportunity to learn more.

Heather Whitestone stepped out on stage in a flowing white dress. For her talent, she was going to do a ballet routine. She seemed to float effortlessly around the stage, leaping to the music with grace and precision. It was an awe-inspiring dance that resulted in a rare standing ovation. It would have been a beautiful performance from anyone, but it was especially impressive because Heather could not hear the music she was dancing to. Heather Whitestone was deaf.

As soon as Mom learned this, she was glued to the screen. She even went so far as to call to my grandparents, who were relaxing downstairs, begging them to come watch. Heather spoke of her passion for ballet, explaining that she'd taken dance lessons as part of her speech therapy at five years old. Heather's mother was a fierce advocate for her daughter and fought to give her all the opportunities she could. The speech therapy Heather underwent was intensive, but it worked, because now she was able to speak and read lips well enough to communicate orally.

Mom's biggest question was whether or not Rachel would be able to speak, so learning this was a revelation for her. If Heather, deaf at eighteen months, could speak and communicate freely, then so could Rachel. Heather was a shining example of all that Rachel could accomplish. If Heather could do it, so could Rachel. Not that my mom needed her deaf daughter to go on national television to talk about her experiences like Heather had. In her wildest dreams, I don't think Mom ever pictured that one day she'd be watching her own child speak about the deaf experience in front of a national audience.

Actually, when I decided to go on *The Bachelor*, I fully expected Mom to be the last person on board. Though she was a fan of the show, she'd always been fairly private, and I just assumed she wouldn't want to see me dating a guy on TV. But, to my surprise, when I called her up to tell her, she was nothing but supportive.

"They've never had a deaf contestant. You might be able to teach a lot of people about cochlear implants," she encouraged me. "If it helps even one family, it's worth it."

At the time, I thought this was just a cliché sentiment Mom was sharing to be supportive. It wasn't until I sat down to write this book and learned of our early lives that I realized just how much Mom meant this. It's exactly what Heather Whitestone did for her. Seeing Heather in the Miss America pageant was a great source of both education and comfort for Mom. It gave her confidence that one day, Rachel would be able to live independently. That was all my mother wanted for her kids, for us to be able to live happy, autonomous lives. Heather proved that hearing loss did not have to hold someone back from communication, independence, and success.

Though it didn't come easy to Heather. When Heather spoke of her childhood and the type of therapy her mother involved her in, it became clear that both Heather and her mom worked very hard for Heather to stay on track developmentally.

Mom was not one to shy away from hard work though. While some may have feared the level of determination it would take to keep Rachel progressing, my mother was assured by it. If hard work was what it would take to ensure Rachel's independence, she would make it happen.

Rachel had many tests and doctor visits ahead of her. It still wasn't clear what level of hearing loss Rachel had. While she likely had more than moderate hearing loss, it could be categorized as either *severe* or *profound*. From my mother's research, she knew that profound hearing loss meant speaking would be incredibly difficult, so she continued to hope that Rachel was in the severe category. Mom would frequently read about what people with severe hearing loss were able to accomplish, and assure herself that Rachel could meet those same milestones.

Of course, that isn't exactly how it works. At the time, Mom had the same mentality that I run into pretty regularly as a deaf person. People tend to assume that all disabilities present the same way in different people, and that if one person with a disability can accomplish something, everyone else can too. But that isn't my personal experience. Even if Rachel did only have severe hearing loss, and other people in the severe category could speak, it didn't mean Rachel would.

Rachel and I have the same level of hearing loss, we both have cochlear implants, and we even share the same genetics. But the way each of us processes and handles our disability is profoundly different. Rachel took to her cochlear implant quickly and easily, but I fought it every step of the way. She loved wearing her implant, which we both lovingly call our "ear," and would wear it as much as possible. But I've always been eager to take mine off at the end of the day.

Growing up, people frequently expected that we would have the same needs or hit the same milestones, but we were two different people processing the same condition. There are so many factors that go into how an individual will respond to their disability, and how they'll approach life with this disability. No condition is cookie-cutter. Mom would learn this very well as she watched us both develop.

Still, there was a comfort in believing that if Rachel was diagnosed in the severe category, she could achieve an expected set of milestones. The first step was to get her fitted for hearing aids and see if that improved what Rachel could hear.

The audiologist encouraged my mom to bring a camera to the fitting appointment, sharing heartwarming stories of overjoyed parents watching their child hear for the first time. People share videos like this with me all the time, and I'm always reluctant to watch them because that wasn't my experience at all, and it wasn't Rachel's. Mom arrived at the appointment full of hope, eager to see the smile on Rachel's face when she heard sound for the first time. She sat with the camera, grinning, eyes wide as the aids were turned on.

But there was no reaction from Rachel—nothing at all.

"Well, Rachel might need to wear them awhile in order to hear something," the audiologist told her. "They don't work like glasses, necessarily. She may need to practice. I'd give it some time."

Mom left that appointment with Rachel still hopeful, but more confused than ever. It was an early lesson in that universal truth: disability follows no pattern of expectations. The same hearing aids that allowed another child with hearing loss to experience noises for the first time were not going to work the same for Rachel. Of course, this sparked more questions as to whether Rachel was going to be able to speak or read the lips of those who were speaking to her. Heather Whitestone utilized a hearing aid to make out rudimentary sounds, which seemed to help her greatly with communication.

But my mother did her best not to dwell on the what-ifs. There was no time for her to wonder what Rachel's future would be. She was too busy trying to introduce the building blocks for that future.

There were three different paths the audiologist presented to my mother on how to move forward with Rachel's language development. They could prioritize teaching her sign language, communicating almost solely through sign. Or there was the oral path, which would focus on speaking to Rachel verbally. Mom could also choose to do a combination of both.

There was value in each choice but, for my mom, the decision was easy. She wanted Rachel to be able to speak to her neighbors, family, friends, the people who were going to be interacting with her regularly. The community around Rachel was hearing, and my mom didn't want Rachel to be ostracized from that community.

Of course, taking the oral route didn't simply mean talking to Rachel and expecting her to understand what was going on around her. My mom developed a very steady daily routine, which included picture books to show Rachel what they would be doing next. If they were going to visit my grandparents, my mother would show her a photo of their house. When Rachel wanted to go to the park, she could point to a photo of the park.

Taking this route resulted in Rachel learning to lip-read very early. At times, my mom would forget that Rachel had to see her mouth to understand what she was saying, and little Rachel would put both of her chubby toddler hands on my mom's cheeks and force her to look directly into Rachel's eyes while she spoke.

Every day was a learning experience with Rachel. And if that wasn't stressful enough, it wasn't just Rachel's diagnosis that my mom was contending with. She was already a few months pregnant with me when she learned that Rachel could not hear.

Thankfully, Mom had fairly easy pregnancies. Many days, her pregnancy was a welcome distraction. If she noticed herself obsessing about Rachel's situation, she would shift her focus to preparing for me.

Knowing that Rachel was going to be delayed by at least a year on her language development, Mom had a lot of hope that I'd be a great language partner for Rachel. We would be a year and a half apart, meaning that I could be learning to talk the same time Rachel was. I would be her buddy on her hearing loss journey.

And I was. But not in the way my parents imagined.

Chapter 2

My mom had no reason to suspect I would have hearing loss like my sister. She'd been explicitly told by one physician that it wasn't something she needed to worry about, so for the duration of her pregnancy, she didn't. Instead, she focused her attention on Rachel and what she could do to make her life more accessible. Because she'd always had easy pregnancies, it wasn't hard to keep her attention on Rachel...until the day of my birth.

My biological dad drove Mom to the hospital, and they arrived at 9:00 a.m. With Rachel, Mom had a long labor and was prepared for the same with me. She figured she'd breathe through her contractions for a while before getting her epidural. But I was born before lunch, leaving no time for an epidural. Despite it being so quick, without the epidural it was a lot more painful than Rachel's birth had been. But none of that mattered to her once she held me in her arms. There was nothing but the pure joy of meeting me for the first time.

The nurses came in to examine me, but my mom wasn't worried when they started the hearing test. It was simply a precaution on behalf of Rachel's condition, nothing to worry about.

But just like Rachel, I failed my initial screening.

This time around, Mom didn't panic or catastrophize. There was no sadness or waves of stress like when she heard about Rachel's deafness. The only emotion that came over her was a surprising one: relief.

As unusual as that may sound, relief is a common emotion felt by many parents in the capital-D Deaf community, a term used to describe people who are typically born deaf and use ASL to communicate. There is a distinction between being Deaf with a capital D, and being deaf as I am. Since I have a cochlear implant and speak orally, I consider myself a member of the lowercase-d deaf community.

Capital D families that predominantly use ASL are often excited to learn that their children are deaf too. That's probably confusing to most able-bodied people, but the Deaf community doesn't consider hearing loss to be a disability any more than you'd consider someone who speaks Spanish disabled. It's simply their language and culture, and knowing their children will integrate into that culture seamlessly is a comfort.

Though my mom wasn't deaf, she experienced this same comfort on behalf of Rachel. Up until this point, Mom imagined

Rachel would be alone in her deafness, isolated by her experiences. Even her siblings wouldn't be able to fully understand her, and the idea of Rachel ever feeling lonely was heartbreaking to Mom. Though she would do anything to make sure Rachel never felt alone, as a hearing mother, there was only so much she could do.

Now, Mom would never have to worry about Rachel being alone. When my family assumed I'd be hearing, they hoped I'd be a language-learning partner for Rachel, but I would become a partner in much more than that.

On top of the relief that Rachel would not be alone, Mom already felt well acquainted with the process I would now undergo. There was so much uncertainty around Rachel's hearing loss that my mom didn't have with me. She was ready to take on this journey for the both of us.

In the two weeks after my birth, Mom found herself wondering if I'd have moderate, severe, or profound hearing loss, just as she had wondered with Rachel. The hearing tests conducted in the hospital were only rudimentary, so we didn't have any clear answers about my hearing loss yet. We would have to wait for a more definitive test.

My mom spent that period of waiting snapping her fingers around my ears, focusing in to see if there was anything in my environment I appeared to hear. Adjusting to a newborn in the house was hard enough, but on top of that, she was constantly observing me for even the slightest recognition of noise.

As an infant, I was too young to do the type of hearing tests that Rachel had done, so I needed to undergo an auditory brain-stem response test. This test would allow the audiologist to look at the response of the brain stem to noise, instead of focusing on my physical reaction to sound. But during the test, I wasn't supposed to move.

"You'll have to make sure she's able to sleep through the appointment," the receptionist explained to my mom when she booked the appointment. "If she doesn't, we won't be able to get the results we need and you'll have to come back."

Waiting even one more week to learn about the state of my hearing loss sounded like agony to Mom. It was always the what-ifs that caused her the most stress, so she was determined to make sure the audiologist got the results they needed. On the day of my appointment, she withheld my nap, then fed and changed me at the doctor's office right before my appointment, hoping I'd fall asleep.

Thankfully, I did, and electrodes were placed on my head and behind my ears. I slept soundly as they recorded my brain's reaction to a variety of sound frequencies. But there wasn't much of a reaction for them to record.

I was likely severely or profoundly deaf as Rachel was, but Mom felt a sense of security knowing she finally had a straight-forward answer. She was going to set me on the same path as she had Rachel. Her only focus was on what to do next to best serve my needs.

By two months old, I had hearing aids, a resource Rachel didn't get until she was over a year old. Initially, this thrilled Mom. Surely getting started early would allow me to pick up language more quickly.

But I hated those hearing aids. They weren't a great fit for my ears to begin with, because my infant ears were too soft. They were always slipping off. And if they weren't slipping off, I was pulling them off. My mom was steadfast about the both of us using our hearing aids as much as possible though, so she stayed consistent despite my resistance.

With the hearing aids in, Mom strived to provide as much enrichment as possible. Frequently, she would pack me up in my stroller and take us to Eugene Airport to listen to the planes take off. The single-terminal airport was only fifteen minutes from our house, so it wasn't unlike taking us to the park.

We'd stand behind the chain-link fence that separated the parking lot from the runway. Rachel would have a little snack of Goldfish crackers, while I sat calmly in the stroller, and we'd wait for the next plane to take off.

I was still a little young to properly react to the planes, but every time one of them would rise into the air, Rachel would buzz with excitement. Her little face would light up, and she'd clap as the plane rose into the sky.

My mom could never be completely sure whether Rachel

enjoyed the view of the plane or liked the rumble against her toddler feet, but she liked to think it was so exciting because Rachel
could pick up the sound with her hearing aids. So this became a
regular part of our weekly routine. Rachel would make the sign
for *plane* any time she wanted to visit the airport.

Rachel knew about two hundred different words in sign language. Although my mom was still leaning into the oral route
of learning language, at a certain point it became clear Rachel
needed to communicate further. So my mom taught her simple
signs to allow her to express her needs.

But those signs never felt like enough for the level of communication Rachel was striving for. Because focusing on the oral route
meant using limited sign language, it didn't take long for Rachel to
run out of ways to convey what she wanted. When it came time
to potty train Rachel, and she struggled to tell Mom when she did
and didn't need to use the bathroom, my mom knew they needed
to take further steps to help Rachel speak.

To learn more about what could be done to help Rachel talk,
we took a trip down to Southern California to visit the John Tracy
Center, a leading organization for children with hearing loss that
provides support worldwide and an amazing resource for my
family. My mom and grandparents visited a lot of different orga-
nizations through the years, but it was the John Tracy Center
that left the greatest impact on our lives. Though far from us, this
center was close to my biological father's parents, so we'd go visit
them and get Rachel scheduled for her appointments.

Mom was ever the optimist about what Rachel could accomplish in terms of language acquisition. So when Rachel sat down for another hearing test with her audiologist, Kathleen, Mom expected to learn about the next steps they needed to take in order for Rachel to learn verbal language. Rachel wore her hearing aids and sat in another enclosed room for the exam while Mom and Kathleen stood in the hallway. My mom was still wearing a smile on her face at the end of the test, but when Kathleen turned to her, she did not share that smile.

"Rachel will never be able to speak," Kathleen told my mom bluntly.

Mom's face fell. "What?" My mother was completely stunned, if not a bit indignant.

"With the level of hearing loss that Rachel has, the hearing aids will not allow her to learn oral language."

My normally mild-mannered mother was not filled with sadness, but with anger. What did Kathleen know about what Rachel was capable of? A hearing test didn't tell Kathleen how hard my mom was willing to work to develop Rachel's language skills. There was no assessment that could say how much Rachel would fight to learn to talk.

Some might call the reaction denial, but for my mom, it was determination. Rachel was going to talk. And hearing Kathleen say she couldn't would change nothing. Mom rejected this as an option.

"Rachel is going to learn to speak," my mom told Kathleen, confident as ever.

But Kathleen wouldn't budge. "No. She isn't. Not with the hearing aids. They aren't providing her with the sound she needs to learn language."

My mom was ready to argue further, but Kathleen's next sentence left her speechless.

"I think Rachel might be the perfect candidate for a cochlear implant."

It was the first time Mom had heard of a cochlear implant. The device was new, but essentially, it was an implant with an external component that could be worn like a hearing aid. Rachel would need a surgical procedure that connected the inner part of the device to the cochlear nerve, allowing the outer part of the device to pick up sounds in Rachel's environment. Basically, a cochlear implant would bypass the ear entirely, and send sound frequencies straight to Rachel's brain.

It wouldn't work exactly like a functioning ear. Cochlear implants are far more limited in the number of frequencies that can be picked up and transmitted to the brain. But it would certainly allow for much more sound than Rachel was getting from the hearing aids.

After explaining how the implant worked, Kathleen took my mom to the nursery where she could watch toddlers who'd already received cochlear implants. John Tracy had a preschool for deaf children with a specialized focus on helping them communicate more effectively. With Rachel in tow, Mom was allowed to walk into a preschool classroom and witness the cochlear implant in action.

There was a certain magic in being able to see children with profound hearing loss use words to communicate with their teachers. The children were running about, stacking blocks and molding Play-Doh. At first glance, it might have looked like a normal nursery. But these were deaf children who were talking to their teachers verbally. And those teachers appeared to have very high expectations of the students. They would ask students to verbalize their needs, even going so far as to ask them to repeat the pronunciation of certain words if they sounded off. Not only were these kids talking; they were being pushed to hone their language skills. If they wanted Play-Doh, they had to correctly pronounce the word *ball*. If the pronunciation wasn't up to their standards, the teachers would sit and patiently wait as the kids kept trying.

I can imagine how my mom felt, because I got to experience this magic myself in 2022 when I visited the John Tracy Center. I already know how cochlear implants work, but watching three-year-olds in the preschool talk and interact happily with each other was indescribable. It nearly brought me to tears witnessing just how far they could come. And I know that's the future Mom was imagining for me and Rachel.

"I am confident that with hearing aids alone, Rachel will never learn to speak. But if you decide to get her a cochlear implant, this is what she'll be capable of." As harsh as Kathleen had been earlier, she now offered Mom something priceless: hope. Hope that her girls were going to have all the opportunities and access to the world that she always dreamed they would.

Though it was jarring to hear that Kathleen didn't believe Rachel would speak, it was the harsh truth Mom needed to hear. It pushed her to accept that the cochlear implant was the right choice. Now, it was the only choice. If this was the device that would allow her daughters to talk, she was all in.

People are often surprised to hear that Mom had no doubts about the surgery. A lot of parents might hesitate at the words *surgical procedure*, but Mom had a familiarity with surgery that most people didn't, with my grandfather being a general surgeon. He too was excited about the idea, along with my granny and biological father.

There were some guidelines that Rachel had to meet before surgery though. The U.S. Food and Drug Administration (FDA) was allowing kids as young as two years old to get cochlear implants, but they had to be profoundly deaf and get little to no benefit from a hearing aid. Rachel met those standards, so she began a battery of cognitive and psychological testing. Though it was never fully explained to my mom what they were evaluating, she assumed they wanted to make sure Rachel had no other cognitive impairments that might prevent her from picking up language.

Once she passed the cognitive tests, she had to be sedated while the anatomy of her ear was examined to make sure the cochlear implant would fit. The implant Rachel and I had, the Nucleus 22, would insert twenty-two electrodes directly into the cochlea. Rachel would then wear what looked like a hearing aid with a coil on the back that could magnetically connect to the internal part of the device.

It was determined that the anatomy of her ear was compatible with the device, and she was scheduled to have surgery at the Oregon Health & Science University in Portland, a little less than two hours from our home in Eugene. That meant my parents had to get a hotel to stay at before surgery.

The morning of Rachel's surgery, Mom had no fear. She was too busy thinking of all the possibilities that were to come. In a few short weeks, Rachel might actually hear the words Mom spoke—something Mom never even dreamed was possible when Rachel was diagnosed as profoundly deaf. Driving to the university hospital, Mom was all smiles.

But that smile faded in the exam room.

A nurse used a tongue depressor and a small flashlight to examine the back of Rachel's throat. "It's inflamed," the nurse said blankly.

"What?" Mom asked, unsure of what that meant or why it mattered.

The nurse took out the tongue depressor and stood from where she was crouching. "It looks like Rachel has a sore throat."

"But she seems fine," Mom said, looking to Rachel.

The nurse just shook her head slowly. "She probably caught a virus. We won't be able to do the surgery if she's sick."

Mom's heart sank. It was only a minor setback, but it hurt like something more. They'd driven all the way to Portland for the surgery, and now the hope of Rachel being able to hear was pushed even further into the distance. After all the testing it took to get to this point, the delay was a huge disappointment.

But eventually Rachel got better, and her surgery was rescheduled. Mom prepared Rachel by showing her picture books about children undergoing surgery—one of which was made especially for Rachel. Communicating with her granddaughter through custom picture books was one of my granny's unique skills. It was a little more difficult to make your own picture books in the nineties, when photographs were made with actual film and had to be developed before you could print them. But still, Granny would have pictures printed and arrange them in booklets for Rachel. The book she created about the cochlear implant surgery explained that Rachel would leave the hospital with an owie above her ear and a bandage applied on top. With the help of Granny's books and an early intervention specialist, my mom was able to roughly explain what the experience would be like to her daughter. And Rachel never seemed particularly afraid.

Thankfully, they didn't have to worry about Rachel experiencing any pain. Though she would have a large incision behind her ear, the surgeon would intentionally cut a nerve, causing the area of the incision, as well as part of her face, to go numb. The nerve would eventually heal, and Rachel would get feeling back in a few weeks.

On the rescheduled surgery day, Rachel's exam went off without a hitch, much to my mom's relief. Mom kissed Rachel goodbye as they rolled her off to the surgical suite, and she went to sit with my biological dad in the waiting room, free of fear or hesitation. Again, I'm sure that's difficult for most parents to understand, but Mom grew up with surgery being a fairly routine part of her father's workday. And she knew this was an easy, breezy outpatient procedure with minimal potential side effects.

She had full confidence in her decision. To this day, I get a lot of questions from people who doubt the choice, but she never did.

When Rachel returned from surgery, her face had a flat affect. She wasn't even able to smile. Although my mom knew this would likely happen due to the severed nerve—and it was certainly a better option than Rachel experiencing pain—it still stirred a small wave of anxiety. Would the nerve heal properly? Was Rachel uncomfortable after surgery? Because Rachel couldn't speak, reading the emotions on her face was Mom's only way to understand how Rachel felt, and now that was taken away too.

But despite the difficulties, it was still an exciting day for everyone. My mom was extremely positive about the experience, and Rachel didn't seem to have any stress after the surgery. It was a day of hope. The outpatient surgery was gentle enough that my parents could drive Rachel home from Portland the same day.

But nobody would know for weeks whether the surgery was successful. Rachel had to heal before they could turn the device on. Prior to returning to OHSU for Rachel's follow-up, Mom had her expectations tempered by the surgeon and other audiologists. While much of the population may believe that getting a cochlear implant is as simple as pushing a button to allow a person to hear the same way an able-bodied individual can, that isn't the reality.

Those of us with implants receive a much smaller input of sound waves than a hearing person does, so it's never quite the same as a hearing person's experience. And it takes time for the brain to adjust to these unfamiliar noises. The brain cannot immediately process sounds it has never heard before. Imagine having your eyes closed your entire life, opening them for the first time in front of a table filled with fruit you've never eaten before, and then being asked to identify which fruit is an apple. Obviously, the shape and color of an apple would be a foreign experience to a previously blind person. Sound is no different.

So though my mom was hopeful Rachel would hear, she did her best not to get too excited. The appointment to turn the cochlear implant on would comprise hours and hours of trying to adjust each individual electrode so that it wasn't too overwhelming for Rachel. An adult patient can obviously convey easily whether a sound is uncomfortable. For a two-year-old, that process is a lot longer and more involved.

Mom arrived with Rachel in tow, and the two of them were taken to an exam room, where they were met with the smiling face of Don Plappinger, who would become a family-favorite audiologist technician for years to come.

"Good morning, Rachel. Are you ready to hear some fun sounds?" Don asked with a grin.

But the sounds weren't so fun for Rachel. During the

appointment, the volume of every electrode had to be raised until it was no longer tolerable to Rachel. Which meant the noise had to be increased until Rachel would show signs of frustration, often to the point of crying. Needless to say, this was hard for both Mom and Rachel, and it would've been made much harder by a frustrated technician.

But Don knew how to work magic. He'd keep a box of animal crackers at his side. When Rachel got upset because the noise was too loud, he'd turn it back down to a tolerable level, and then give Rachel an animal cracker to calm her down. She'd relax fairly quickly, and they'd try again.

Even with this technique, though, it was a long process. In the middle of the appointment, Rachel needed a potty break (this was to be expected after hours and hours of testing). Mom took her down a long hallway to an industrial-style bathroom, the kind you usually find in medical facilities. For whatever reason, public toilets always have an inexplicably strong flush, and this was definitely true of the toilets at OHSU. As soon as Mom helped Rachel off the toilet and flushed, Rachel let out a horrible wail. She was bawling, pointing at the toilet in horror.

Public restrooms had never bothered her before, and for a moment, Mom was thrown for a loop. Why was she so scared? And that's when she realized... Rachel could actually hear the sound of the flushing. In her tiny toddler brain, the porcelain white toilet had yelled at her like a monster.

It was the only time Mom was actually happy to hear Rachel

cry. The tears were contagious, as my mom both laughed and cried, pulling Rachel close to comfort her after the monster toilet's attack.

Rachel could hear! For the first time, Mom had proof the implant had worked.

It wasn't the most pleasant first noise to experience, that's for sure. But that was the way of the world. There were a lot of scary noises that Rachel would soon be introduced to. Rachel's young mind couldn't even begin to process all the sounds that existed in the world. But she was finally hearing some of them, able to experience the symphony the world had to offer, with all the splendor and fear that came along with that.

And soon, I would do the same. Seeing Rachel's reaction to sound gave Mom a lot of hope for my future as well. Though Rachel had initially feared the toilet, she seemed to enjoy other noises she experienced that week, bobbing along to the radio in the car and planting herself in front of the TV when it was on. And if Rachel was excited about the sound her new implant provided, surely I would be too.

Except, like I've mentioned, disability is never one-size-fits-all. And my experiences with the cochlear implant were wildly different from Rachel's, as we would very quickly see for ourselves.

Chapter 3

On my second birthday, I got a gift that would transform the rest of my life. My cochlear implant surgery was scheduled at OHSU, so my birthday party was a small affair in our hotel room in Portland. My parents and I celebrated after my pre-op appointment the day before surgery with gifts and a small white cake dotted with colorful icing balloons.

I can't say there's much I remember about my own surgery, being only two years old. But according to my mom, the day was uneventful. The procedure went as smoothly as Rachel's had, and I responded similarly. I couldn't move the muscles in my face and reached for the Band-Aid over my incision, but I wasn't in any pain. And just like Rachel, I was fairly calm about the procedure. At that point, through the eyes of my mother, our hearing loss journeys had been pretty comparable.

But those journeys would soon diverge. Although Rachel was

initially scared by the sound of the toilet flushing, she took very well to the noise coming through her cochlear implant. Rachel had a curiosity about the noises around her and welcomed sound with open arms, like a new friend she was meeting for the first time.

But if sound was Rachel's new friend, it was my tentative acquaintance. When it came time for the appointment to turn my cochlear implant on, I resisted every noise. Testing the volume of each electrode is already a grueling experience, even for children who are excited to hear for the first time. It was especially agonizing for me. Mom had her suspicions that I wasn't as willing to hear as Rachel was, but she chalked up my behavior to an exhausting day. She remained hopeful that after some sleep I'd be more willing to wear my cochlear implant.

I wasn't. Shortly after I woke up the next morning, Mom put on the cochlear implant and turned it on. I tried pulling it off immediately. Mom did her best to stop me.

"We have to keep this on. Come on, Abigail, let's get some cereal." Mom figured she could distract me with breakfast.

Rachel munched her cereal contently, but I chose to forego breakfast and instead walked over to the couch and forced myself back to sleep, even though I'd just woken up. Anyone who's ever been in the proximity of a toddler in the morning knows how weird it is for them to want to sleep right after waking up.

It was a strange reaction, but I'd just had that grueling appointment the day before, so Mom thought I was still tired and needed a little more rest. She let me sleep a bit longer on the couch. And when I got up, she brought me my cochlear implant and turned it on once more.

To her dismay, I gave the same response, forcing myself to lie down and go to sleep as soon as she turned on the implant. It was like my brain couldn't process the sound, so it just shut my body down in response.

My reaction was a far cry from those happy videos you may have seen of deaf children experiencing sound for the first time after having their implants turned on. Because of the popularity of these videos, I think people usually assume that receiving a cochlear implant is a universally joyful experience. It's probably safe to assume that most able-bodied people view hearing as a wonderful gift, one that anyone would be thrilled to receive.

But all my little brain knew was silence. At two years old, sound was not a concept I could fully comprehend. I didn't know what I'd been missing and didn't long for it. So my first experiences with it were nothing short of overwhelming. I wasn't even willing to try.

Mom was thrown for a loop. After her experiences with Rachel, she thought she knew what to expect. Her daughters had the exact same disability and had been raised in the same way, so how much could their experiences really differ? Significantly, as it turned out.

My mom, flustered, called up our audiologist straightaway.

"What are we dealing with here? Rachel never shut down like this. What should I do?" Mom asked.

It wasn't as though she could force me to wear the implant and get used to the device when it was fully within my power to take it off whenever I wanted.

"For now, why don't you turn it down to the lowest sensitivity possible? Let her get adjusted to the implant slowly," the audiologist suggested.

"But will she be able to hear if I turn it down?" Mom asked.

"I think for the moment, the priority should be getting her comfortable with the device. When she resists it less, we can worry about how much she's hearing."

As much as Mom wanted me to hear, she knew it wouldn't happen if I refused to wear the implant. So she turned it down as low as possible. I wore a small body processor on my back, about the size of a cell phone. Using this processor, Mom was able to adjust the sensitivity of the implant.

This helped, though I still resisted wearing the implant, which Mom called my "ear." Mom offered treats as an incentive to wear my ear. She did her best to give me positive reinforcement, but inwardly, the stress was overwhelming. With the device turned so low, she wasn't sure I was hearing anything at all. And if I wasn't, would I reject the implant entirely? What would that mean for my future? Would I be able to acquire language, as Rachel was beginning to?

It took several appointments and a lot of experimentation to get the cochlear implant adjusted just right so that I could hear the world around me without being significantly bothered by it.

I was never forced to wear the device past the point of comfort, since I could always take it off. Both my mom and my doctors made sure I tolerated the implant. But my experience isn't a rare one. Adjusting to sound is a long process. Some children are simply more amenable to that process than others. Sure, I may have been a little out of my comfort zone at times, but not more so than able-bodied children who are pushed out of their comfort zone for their own well-being. The same way you'd encourage a child to eat broccoli for the sake of their health, one floret at a time, my mom encouraged me to use my ear.

Just a few short months later, my relationship to the cochlear implant shifted. I was becoming more open to the sounds around me, though to this day, I probably still have a different relationship with my implant than Rachel does. While I love being able to hear, at the end of the day, I'm quick to take off the implant and unwind in silence.

Unlike my sister, I was never the one to reach for my cochlear implant first thing in the morning. I was far more content to eat my cereal in silence, and slowly wake up before tuning into the sound of the world around me. Noiselessness is a natural state of being for me, and a peaceful one. Because unlike hearing individuals, using my cochlear implant always takes work. Once I put the implant in, I'm putting in some level of effort to integrate noise into my brain. You might hear your fridge running and immediately know what that noise is, but I actually have to sit a moment and try to understand what that humming is, how far away the noise is, if it's a normal sound I hear daily. I'm not complaining about the implant; it's an amazing tool, but that doesn't mean I don't get relief when it's off. Shoes are a useful tool you use to leave your house and enjoy the wider world, but I'm guessing you're pretty grateful to take them off once you get home.

Some people would see Rachel's willingness to accept sound more easily as a positive trait, and it was. But my relationship to sound is also a positive force in my life. Our experiences were just different. Rachel's excitement about hearing propelled her forward at a faster pace than me, but she also struggled in ways I didn't.

When we were a little older, at Christmas, we'd each choose our wishes for Santa Claus. Mom would help us write a letter to the North Pole, and we'd ask for the toys we wanted that year. It was a lighthearted tradition, except for the year that Rachel asked Santa to give her hearing.

I may not have been as open to the implant as Rachel was initially, but I also never wished that I was hearing. Ultimately, I was happy with my cochlear implant, but I didn't need more than that. Both of our lived experiences were valid and came with their own sets of hardship.

Shortly after my surgery, Mom got us into a summer program at Tucker Maxon in Portland. Tucker Maxon is an inclusive school that takes the oral approach to educating children with hearing loss. Because we lived in Eugene, we couldn't go there year-round, but the summer program was the perfect opportunity for my mom to explore the school further.

We all fell in love with it. The preschool at Tucker Maxon was a unique experience in that some days, Rachel and I were in a small classroom of only toddlers with hearing loss. But two days a week, they combined our class with a hearing preschool class that was adjacent to the Tucker Maxon campus. Not only did this allow us to socialize with a larger group of kids, but it put us in an environment where spoken language was more prevalent. The philosophy at Tucker Maxon was that children with hearing loss would do better if they had spoken language models, and by combining the classrooms, our peers would become the models.

The summer program lifted a weight off my mom's shoulders. Until that point, she had been the sole arbiter of our language development. She felt a constant need to be working on our speech in one form or another, so we wouldn't miss out on progress. Dinnertime wasn't just a time to sit down to eat, but to ask us to talk about the food on our plate and reiterate different words. We had to describe the color and texture of our food, enunciating every syllable. Mom had become real chatty, talking nonstop during car rides so we'd be immersed in language as much as possible. Being a parent was hard enough, but to be our teacher 24–7 added another layer of stress.

With Tucker Maxon, she was able to drop us off and know that we were being provided with essential learning experiences. Finally, she had the freedom to let go a little. And it gave her an excellent community of parents who were going through the same situation as our family, which Mom never had before.

It only made sense that we'd move to Portland so we could attend the school full time. My grandparents were retired so they could easily follow, and my biological dad's job was flexible. He agreed to get an apartment in Portland, and we were all but ready to move into it when my parents' relationship began to deteriorate.

My parents' divorce was in the works before we even left for Portland. So we moved without him. If I'm being honest, I don't remember much about my biological father. I was so young when he left us, so it wasn't a huge factor in my life.

But it was hard for Mom, though she never showed that to us. She never envisioned herself as a single parent. At the time, she was a stay-at-home mom, so my grandparents stepped up to help out financially. Shortly after we moved to Portland, they got a condo in Vancouver, Washington, and we moved in with them there. Though technically in another state, Vancouver is considered a suburb of Portland, just a bridge away. From the edge of Oregon, you'd be able to see Vancouver across the Columbia River, so the drive to school wasn't bad.

The support of my grandparents became a vital pillar in Mom's life. Though I was too young to understand it at the time, they uprooted their entire lives to help us. They'd volunteer in our preschool classroom and were extremely involved in our education. With their help, Mom was able to get a job. Granny and Grandpa would pick us up and drop us off from preschool while Mom worked. They acted more like parents than grandparents, becoming primary caretakers for us, in addition to my mom. I don't know how we would've survived this time without them.

Mom took a job at the Vancouver Children's Therapy Center. With her degree in counseling, it was a good fit, though probably not one she would've initially chosen for herself. But after her experiences with her own daughters, she felt called to help others adjust to caring for disabled children.

At the clinic, Mom was one of the first staff members that families would meet if a child was flagged for further evaluation. After the therapists evaluated the patients, my mom would take their results and guide the parents through the next steps, helping them get the resources they needed. There was a lot of paperwork to deal with, which was overwhelming for parents who were dealing with disability for the first time in their life. Mom helped make this journey a little easier.

And it was a very rewarding job. Most of the time, parents were relieved to get a diagnosis for their child and begin the process of seeking help. Of course, a lot of the time that diagnosis came with a fair amount of uncertainty. This was something Mom knew well.

Even while at Tucker Maxon, there was a lot of uncertainty about what our future looked like in terms of language development. We were thriving at school, learning every day, and making friends. The both of us were excited to go into class each morning and came home equally happy. Still, the cochlear implant was a new technology, and to what degree we'd be able to hear and speak was still a mystery.

My mom dealt with that uncertainty by always providing a rich language-learning environment. No matter how simple a task, it was an opportunity to teach us. Even something as routine as riding my Barbie bike on the sidewalk became a language-learning experience.

"What color is your bike?" Mom would ask as I was walking it from the garage to the sidewalk.

"Pink!" I'd answer eagerly.

"And what's the weather like today?" Mom would immediately follow up.

"Summy!" My pronunciation was a little off in my early years, as you might have expected from a child a year or two younger than I was. It took time for my language development skills to catch up.

But Mom's constant inquisition helped to keep me talking, because I wasn't the kind of kid who would talk on my own.

Speaking came a little easier to Rachel, who was more easily attuned to the world around her. Rachel loved cooperative play. If there was a chance for her to play with other kids or our family members, she'd take it. A favorite activity at our house was playing Airplane, a game in which we'd line up chairs from the kitchen table and everyone would take a paper ticket from Rachel before taking our seats. Then Rachel would fly the plane, which gave her an opportunity to describe where they were going or what the sky looked like outside of their imaginary windows. These communal activities excited Rachel the most, and they heavily leaned on language.

I was more solitary. I preferred a coloring book, puzzles, or Legos to dramatic play. Mom worried a little more about my development because it was harder to push language into solitary activities, and I was far more independent in my activities than my sister.

Still, Mom did her best to trust the process and knew that each of us was set to succeed at our own pace. My mom knew I was smart; despite her fears, she was sure I'd pick things up eventually.

When parents would come into her center, worried about what the future held for their children, Mom shared the piece of wisdom that carried her through our journeys.

"Whatever happens, everything is going to be okay. Your child will grow, and the future may look different from what you imagined, but they will find their place in the world."

Nothing is scarier than the fear of the unknown, especially for Mom, who drew comfort from careful planning. But plans fall apart. So, when her plans for a successful marriage and smooth parenting journey fell apart, Mom had to find another source of comfort. She leaned into the knowledge that whoever we became, we would contribute to our communities in our own way. There would be bumps in the road, frustrations, and stress, but regardless of the circumstances, everyone has something to offer the world.

Rachel and I used to tease my mom for how often she'd say that we all had something to offer. She'd repeat this phrase constantly. But it's a universal truth, and an important one for the disabled community. In a world that prioritizes conventional success and independence, it's so easy to feel like disability is a burden that inhibits that independence. For years, I struggled to fit into my community and longed for the type of belonging that came so easily to able-bodied people. But through my hearing loss, I've given something different to the world than my able-bodied friends and family. What kind of world would it be if we didn't have an array of unique perspectives to learn about and appreciate?

Mom always knew this, and it carried her through her difficult divorce. In the first few years of my life, our circumstances changed so rapidly, but we were able to find joy in even the most difficult moments. Moving in with my grandparents as a single mom may not have been in Mom's plans, but I cherish that time the five of us had together.

Because as much as life had already shifted, more change was on the horizon. Soon, we'd be moving not just out of my grandparents' town house, but out of the state entirely. Our family was changing, and yet again, it was for the better.

Chapter 4

H ello?" Granny answered the phone while Rachel and I
fussed in the background. Dinnertime was nothing short
of chaotic at our house, and as usual, Mom was trying to get us
to eat.

"Suzie, it's for you!"

Mom kept a careful eye on us as she walked to the phone,
mildly annoyed to have to deal with a call during this hour.

"Hello?" she answered, eyes periodically darting back to the
dinner table, where Rachel was refusing her vegetables.

"Suzie, hi, it's Weston."

"Weston, hello," Mom replied shortly.

"How are you?"

"I'm good."

"That's great. I was hoping you'd had a great week."

Mom didn't have time for small talk and was a bit annoyed

that this conversation didn't seem to be going anywhere. "We're actually in the middle of dinner right now. Was there something you needed to ask me?"

If Weston was taken aback by the question, he didn't show it. "Yes, actually. I'd like to ask you to dinner."

They had met a couple of weeks prior at a country club wedding. My mom was the bridesmaid of an old sorority sister. Rachel and I were flower girls, though we didn't stay for the whole wedding. It would've been a long day for the two of us, so my grandparents took us home and allowed my mom a rare evening with her girlfriends.

Weston was a cousin of the groom. A dental student at the time, he was an eligible bachelor, and some of the older attendees encouraged him to mingle. One woman in particular, Emily Brooks, was both an alumna of the same sorority as my mom and the wife of a dentist. So she knew people on both the bride and groom's sides, including Weston and his father. She approached Weston to point out the table where Mom had been seated.

"You should go over there. Those are all Tri Deltas, and I think they're all single. But avoid the redhead. She's already got two kids."

Thankfully, Weston wasn't great at taking unsolicited advice. While everyone was waiting for the toasts, he took a glass of champagne to my mom and introduced himself.

At the time, another man was hounding Mom. He'd had way too much to drink and no matter how much she tried, she could not get out of the obnoxious conversation. Weston waited patiently as this near stranger talked mom's ear off.

"Would it be alright if I asked for your number?" Weston asked when the other man finally retreated.

He was handsome, polite, and there was some chemistry from the start.

"I suppose that would be fine," she answered and gave it to him.

But she didn't expect anything to come of it. After my dad left, she had no interest in dating. How would she even have the time? We were a full-time job, on top of the part-time job she had. Her focus was on us.

So when he called and asked for a date, it caught her off guard. But she quickly agreed to a simple cup of coffee and then hurried off the phone to get back to the dinner table.

For any single mother, dating is a juggling act. Mom had to balance her job, caring for her kids, and entertaining the possibility of a relationship. So, from the very first date, she took a no-nonsense approach.

The time they spent together was intentional, void of any small talk, but Weston wasn't intimidated by this. It took a while for my mom to feel serious enough about the relationship to introduce us to him, and when she finally did, it was only as a friend. But the time we all spent together was so natural.

Rachel was five, had forged a social life for herself, and was often getting invited to birthdays or playdates. My mom would schedule coffee dates during these times, bringing me along with some of the memory games I loved so much. Weston would play them with me.

I'd take my little cards, which had an array of items drawn on them. An apple, a cloud, a tennis ball. Each of the items had two cards, and I'd arrange them in a square grid on the table, then flip them over and find the matching counterpart.

Weston and I would take turns. I'd find two apples, and then he'd have to find a cloud and would instead flip over a tennis ball. I can say with pride I won every single memory game, mostly because Weston knew I was competitive and I'd get annoyed if he beat me. He would talk to my mom, pretend not to remember which card had a red apple hiding on the other side, and we all had a great time.

Their relationship progressed. When Weston came over, he didn't just spend his time with my mom. Rachel and I loved to play chase, and he'd take us to the park across the street and run around the playground with us. In retrospect, it's hard to imagine running through a jungle gym with two toddlers was a great date night activity. But he seemed to enjoy it all the same, and we definitely enjoyed him.

Watching Weston win over our affection sold Mom on the relationship. She'd been falling for him since the day they met, but it wasn't until she could see us all together that she knew this would actually work long term. And once they both decided they were in it for the long haul, they wasted no time getting engaged.

They spent a big chunk of their time dating long distance prior to the wedding. Weston had to do a general practice rotation in Oklahoma City. After that, he'd be starting his residency in Cleveland, which left a brief window to have the wedding in Oregon.

It was a modest affair, no frills, held in Weston's Presbyterian church. They were paying for the wedding themselves and had little money to spare. Though, even disregarding their financial situation, neither of them wanted a fancy wedding. They had their hearts set on the life they were about to build together, not the wedding day itself.

Rachel and I wore cute flower girl dresses, and when it came time to exchange vows, we stood by Mom's side. After vowing to be there for Mom in good times and bad, sickness and in health, Weston turned to me and Rachel to make the same promises. He would always be there for us, no matter what. And I can honestly say he stuck to those vows.

Mom wore a wedding ring that had Weston's birthstone, peridot. As if his promises to Rachel and I weren't already cute enough, he got us each peridot necklaces to match Mom's ring. He knew he wasn't just marrying Mom, but marrying into this family, and he made every effort to show it. Though it was a quiet occasion, the wedding solidified what Mom already knew: she made the right choice when she agreed to marry him.

Rachel and I stayed with my grandparents the week after the wedding. Mom and Weston packed and moved everything to our new home in Cleveland, where Weston had his dental residency. It would be the last time we'd see our grandparents for a while, since we were moving so far away.

It was an adjustment at first. Granny and Grandpa dropped us off in Cleveland on their way to Scotland, and it was hard to say goodbye. We had to go from living with them every single day, essentially having them as second parents, to a brand-new family structure.

Though Mom and Weston would've preferred to remain in the Portland area and knew they would return, Cleveland ended up being the perfect adventure for our new little family. As Mom would say, sometimes the best plans are ones you don't make. Life had thrust us into this new city, but Mom found an amazing auditory verbal school in Mayfield, a suburb of Cleveland. We got a house there, so Weston could commute easily. It was a tiny little rental, only nine hundred square feet, but it kept us close as we all adjusted to this life change.

It wasn't as hard of an adjustment as Mom thought it would be, considering how young we were. We missed Granny and Grandpa at first, but that got overshadowed by our excitement to go out and make friends. And we were lucky enough to make some fantastic ones.

Rachel and I became especially close with a set of siblings, Sarah and Danny, who also had cochlear implants. Danny and

Rachel were close to the same age and had very similar milestones in terms of their speech and hearing. Though Rachel had always pretty easily found friends, Mom worried about me being more reserved.

I preferred isolated play to group activities. I wasn't one to speak up if I needed something, like Rachel always did. But Sarah, who was my age, had a similar personality. She was equally as reserved, and somehow that resulted in us becoming fast friends.

For so many disabled kids, there is a limited pool of potential friends. Being behind on our language development, it was easier for Rachel and me to make friends within the hearing-loss community, but that meant a smaller pool of potential companions. So often, disabled people end up making friendships of convenience, even if personalities clash. And there isn't anything wrong with that. I've got a lot of friends who are my exact opposites. But that wasn't the situation with Sarah.

Sarah was a friend I would've made regardless of our shared hearing loss, because we were so naturally similar. When going through this drastic life change, it was especially nice to find a friend who was both complementary to me *and* shared my disability. I don't think I've found a friend like that before or since meeting Sarah. I spent most of my time with her or at home with my new family.

And that family soon grew. My parents knew they wanted more kids—and neither of them had any qualms about having more deaf children. Most of my mom's fears surrounding our hearing loss revolved around the unknown, but she could see that with the cochlear implants, our language skills would develop, which was always her greatest concern. With that out of the way, there were no doubts she could guide another deaf child through the journey of language acquisition.

But we still didn't know what condition caused our hearing loss. There are a variety of genetic disorders that result in deafness. One in particular, Usher syndrome, resulted in not just loss of hearing, but eventually loss of vision as well. That was the one fear that still lingered for Mom, the possibility that we may go blind in addition to being deaf. And it was a possibility Mom wanted to prepare for before they had any more kids.

So when Mom became pregnant with my little brother, Alistair, they underwent genetic testing to make sure Usher syndrome was not responsible for our hearing loss.

There's a lot of controversy around genetic testing. I've been asked if I'd do genetic testing to see if any of my children would be deaf, and I wouldn't. But I'm in an entirely different situation than Mom was when she got pregnant with Alistair. She still didn't know the cause of our hearing loss, and therefore she still didn't fully know the ramifications. It wouldn't have made any difference to my mom what our genetic condition was. She would've had Alistair regardless. But Mom wanted the full spectrum of information so she could properly plan to help her children.

And if I didn't know what caused my condition, I might feel the same about my future kids. But because of the genetic testing my parents did, I know that my hearing loss was caused by a gene mutation that impacts a protein called Connexin 26. Without adequate supply of this protein, potassium in the inner ear becomes too high and leads to profound deafness. It does not cause any other health conditions. Knowing this, I don't see any reason to do genetic testing for my future kids. I'm well prepared to handle them being deaf, and I don't see it as a condition I need to avoid. Neither did Mom and Weston. Again, Mom is a strong believer that we all have a place in the world. There is no person that doesn't deserve to be here, and I agree with her.

They also learned that Weston did not have the gene that caused the Connexin 26 mutation, so Alistair would be hearing.

By the time Mom gave birth to Alistair, Rachel and I were in the first and second grades, and were nothing but excited about the prospect of a new baby in the house. We were old enough to process the news fully, and thankfully, Alistair was a really calm baby. He didn't cry much, which gave us a lot of opportunities to play with him.

Though Rachel and I couldn't really comprehend that Alistair was hearing. When we played with him, we'd do some of the same things we learned in preschool, like to enunciate our words slowly. Or we'd go up to him and hold his head very gently, so he was looking straight at our faces when we talked to him. Instead of reading to Alistair by sitting next to him, we'd be across from him so he could see our faces. But at least he got some very helpful language acquisition tools, even if they weren't altogether necessary.

After Weston finished his residency, we set out to move back home. While planning our move back to Oregon, logistic fears came into play. Weston was Alistair's biological dad, but if anything ever happened to my mom, Weston wouldn't have any legal standing to claim guardianship of us. By this time, it had been years since we were in contact with our biological father. It only seemed right that Weston would formally adopt us. Rachel and I had already been calling Weston our dad for a while. We didn't need paperwork to know we were a family.

Though we did get excited once the adoption was finalized. The next day at school, I made an unexpected proclamation to my class.

"Yesterday, I got adopted!" my seven-year-old self announced cheerily.

This garnered a few weird looks from everyone in the room, including my teacher.

"You were adopted? By who?" Mrs. Yarrow asked me.

"My dad!" I answered, as if this should've been obvious.

That answer didn't exactly clear things up. Mrs. Yarrow wasn't sure if I'd been in foster care and would now move in with a new family. That was an interesting call home, but Mom had a good laugh about it.

Alistair was seven months old by the time we moved back to Oregon. Though moving to Cleveland had been easy, moving away was a little harder. We were older now and a lot more attached to the great friends we'd made. And while we did our best to keep in touch, living out of state meant we wouldn't be seeing them much.

But it was great to have our grandparents back in our lives—even though our new community looked a lot different from what we had in Ohio.

In Ohio, we had access to the hearing-loss community in a big way, especially because our school was *designed for* kids with hearing loss. In Portland, we used to have Tucker Maxon, but they were just barely developing their elementary school classes. Which meant it was time for us to attend public school with able-bodied kids.

We went to Candalaria Elementary, a highly rated school in Salem. Rachel took to it quickly. Not only was she more naturally extroverted than me, but being a year ahead, she was more advanced in her language development too. And, as would become a common theme in our lives, Rachel was willing to speak up for herself. I was not.

I never made much of a fuss. I'd sit in class quietly, comprehending what I could, which wasn't much. Being thrust into public school meant having a huge communication barrier. It didn't just limit what I was able to process from my teacher, it also impacted my young social life. Though even if I was able-bodied, it still would've been difficult for me to make friends at Candalaria. I was a quiet kid, and most of the other students had all grown up together. They lived in the same neighborhoods and had been friends since their toddler years. The combination of my introversion, hearing loss, and the fact that friend groups had already formed at Candalaria meant I spent most of my time alone.

It was the first time in my life that I had to face how difficult socializing could be. Some kids could make fast friends, but that was never me. Socializing was more labor intensive than school-work. I loved learning, but I didn't take to school because the social aspect was a hurdle. Communicating didn't come easily to me.

The other kids didn't instinctively understand me, something that hearing individuals take for granted. In a classroom full of kids, it was difficult for me to hear what was going on. For someone with full hearing, it's easy to assess whether someone's voice is coming from right next to you or across the room. With a cochlear implant, though, sound has almost no depth perception. The noise goes into my implant, and I hear it at the same volume, whether it's right next to me or across a room.

Some people assume you get a cochlear implant, and you no longer have a disability, but that just isn't true. Hearing for me was always work. A cochlear implant will never be the same as having a functioning cochlea.

My school did offer speech therapy, but I didn't find it very helpful, and only three children in my grade were taken out of class for it. One of them had a severe stutter, and the other was nearly mute. I was already far exceeding their language acquisition skills, but the speech therapist had to work with all three of us at the same time, which meant that she needed to focus more on the other two students who were struggling more severely. I just didn't get much time with her, and thus my time in speech therapy was wasted. But I still needed the help, and I wasn't getting it.

My teacher, Mrs. Carden, didn't really notice me struggling at Candalaria because I was so quiet. Mom was the first to pick up on the fact that something was wrong.

"How was school?" Mom would ask when she'd pick me up.

"Fine," I'd answer from the back seat of the car.

"What did you learn today?"

"I don't know." I would shrug, then stare at the window, refusing to elaborate. No matter how many times she asked, she couldn't get an answer out of me.

This was a huge red flag for Mom. I'd always loved to learn and would come home and happily share what I'd discovered in class. But I didn't learn much at Candalaria, and Mom could see that. She scheduled a parent–teacher conference to get to the bottom of things.

"I'm not so sure Abigail really understands what is going on in class. I often ask her about her day, and she doesn't have much to say about it," Mom explained.

"Really? Because she does well on all her assignments. And she never says she has any issues hearing." Mrs. Carden was immediately closed off to the idea that there was a problem.

"Yes, well, that's just Abigail's personality. She's not the kind of kid to ask for help. She'd much rather keep to herself."

Mrs. Carden shrugged. "I really think she's doing just fine. She's a pleasure to have in class."

Mom knew then that Candalaria was not a good fit for me, and no amount of talking to my teacher was going to change that.

Of course I was a pleasure to have in class. Even from a young age, I strived to be a pleasure to everyone around me, to my detriment. But that didn't mean I wasn't struggling.

Thankfully, there was another school nearby, Salem Heights, which served as the district center for deaf children and children with hearing loss. As soon as I transferred schools, I felt more comfortable than I ever had at Candalaria. There were many other kids with hearing loss, so I didn't have to struggle as much to be understood.

My new classroom was far more accessible. The desks were in a horseshoe, all facing the teacher, and I could always see the teacher speaking. At Candalaria, they grouped desks in clumps of four, and I often had to strain my neck to see my teacher head-on, which made hearing her more difficult.

We also had a sign-language interpreter in our classroom, which surprisingly I found very helpful. Of course, I didn't know sign language, but the interpreter made it a point to mouth everything the teacher was saying and place emphasis where it mattered. She was theatrical in her facial expressions, and I could lip-read well enough that this was a great help.

Back at Candalaria, I hated music class. I was so aware that with my cochlear implant, I was likely singing out of tune and worried about the judgment of other students. But at Salem Heights, a lot of the kids had the same struggles, and I didn't have to worry about being embarrassed. Finally, I was able to focus on my actual school activities, instead of worrying about what other kids were thinking of me.

With that level of accessibility, I flourished. My personality began to shine, and I was able to make friends pretty easily. I never had to worry about feeling singled out for my disability, because a lot of my peers had similar conditions. At Candalaria, I had a speech and language therapist who would work with me, but I had to be called out of class specifically for our time together. At Salem Heights, everyone had time with a speech therapist, so there was no feeling of being singled out.

Though even with all the added help and new friends, I still always viewed interacting with others as work. My favorite social activities were physical ones. I loved soccer because I could be with friends but not have to sit and talk to anyone. I was always drawn to athletics. Mom jokes that one day she was dropping me off at soccer, and I told her, "I hope they make us run laps today." What was supposed to be a punishment was my solitary dream.

Because socializing was so difficult, I always saw home as a sanctuary. My mom had my youngest brother, Stuart, a few months after I transferred to Salem Heights, and I loved our family of six. Being with my parents and my siblings was the only time I could truly be myself. They understood me. They knew what I struggled with. My brothers had deaf sisters from birth, and they never knew anything different, so all our needs were normalized. While other kids might have been drawn to playdates and weekend sleepovers, I was thrilled to spend my weekends on family activities.

But middle school was quickly approaching. Soon I realized the preteens around me strived to have more autonomy. They wanted to hang out with friends more than their families. Leaving elementary school meant the social gap caused by my hearing loss was going to grow a lot wider. If I wanted to avoid falling behind socially, I was going to need to find a way to fit in.

And the journey to fitting in had a drastic impact on how I viewed my hearing loss.

Chapter 5

M iddle school is a tumultuous time for most people, and my experience was no exception. It's an age of transition, where kids are becoming more independent. The preteen years are a time most people start thinking about who they are as a person and how they want to spend their time.

But it was hard for me to figure out who I was, because I spent my first year of middle school relearning how to hear.

When Rachel and I were approved to get cochlear implants, the recommendation was that children receive only one implant. The surgery could cause all working nerves in the cochlea to die. So if the cochlear implant didn't work, at least only one ear would be impacted and the other ear would still retain whatever function it had.

By the time we reached middle school, we were offered something that was brand-new to the implant community: a second cochlear implant. Younger children were now being encouraged to do two implants instead of just one. I didn't mind the idea, as I had no recollection of what it was like to get my first implant. Our audiologist, Don Plappinger, talked to us about how it might improve what we could hear.

"It adds a lot more depth perception to sound. You'll be able to hear someone call your name from across the cafeteria," he told us.

It was pretty frustrating that I wasn't able to hear people call me from far away. If this helped me with that, I was happy to try.

The surgery itself was easy enough, and I remember it as a pretty uneventful day. I'd recently gotten my tonsils out and was scared that the experience would be similarly painful, but it wasn't. I was in and out quickly with only some stitches and a bandage, and I wasn't in any pain. In fact, I was pretty excited to have a few days off school, relaxing at home and eating McDonalds as a treat. The worst part was not being able to sleep on that side. Overall, surgery was a breeze. But the days to come would be grueling.

I went into the process believing that the surgery would be the worst part. After I healed, I'd turn on my cochlear implant and just listen throughout the day in order to train that ear.

I was sorely mistaken.

With my first implant, I was at the prime age for language development, which made things easier. And until I started writing this book and recounting the early years with my mom, I didn't know just how hard it was to learn with my first implant. I had no memory of that in middle school and wasn't prepared for what the new implant would sound like.

When someone receives a cochlear implant, it isn't as though they can put it on and smooth sound just streams through the device. At first, it sounds almost robotic, with a lot of disruptive clicking noises. I had to actively *try* to hear, and with practice and concentration, my brain slowly became accustomed to the sound.

It was annoying, and I tried to tough it out and force myself to use the new implant, but the difficulty was compounded. I was already having a hard time hearing with my first implant, so a second device was just overwhelming. With the sound of the new implant, it became impossible to hear with my usual ear. Try focusing on a lecture in class when one ear is giving you robotic feedback and random beeping noises. I couldn't concentrate on anything else when I had the new implant in, so I had to dedicate time to using it outside of normal school hours.

On the plus side, this meant I got one class period dedicated to turning my cochlear implant on and learning with it. There was a little pocket in the hallway under the stairs and I'd curl under there with my iPod and watch episodes of *Friends*. Admittedly, watching *Friends* was a lot less fun when struggling to hear, but it was still a perk. Kids would walk by and wonder why I was allowed to watch shows in the middle of the school day, and I'd keep the reason to myself.

"Aren't you supposed to be in class right now?" random teachers would pass by and ask me.

"I'm supposed to be using this period to turn on my new cochlear implant," I'd explain.

Being such a rule follower, I got a bit of joy about breaking the rules without *actually* breaking the rules. But the one hour a day I got to watch *Friends* wasn't enough to make genuine progress with the implant. It took hours and hours with the implant for any real improvement, and I didn't have that kind of spare time.

Ultimately, I decided the second implant wasn't for me. I was doing fine with my first one, and whatever benefit I'd get from the second wasn't worth the difficulty.

My mom often gets asked why she didn't just wait until we were older and could decide for ourselves that we wanted the cochlear implant, since a lot of Deaf people choose not to get one. But I am eternally grateful she made that decision for me before I could. Getting my cochlear implant when I was actively learning language made the process so much easier than trying to learn in my middle school years. To get my first cochlear implant later in life would've been extremely disruptive. I'm not even sure I'd be successful with it, or how long it would take even if I was. But my cochlear implant has become so central to how I live my life. I can't fathom life without one.

Even as an adult, I've never tried to wear my second implant. That's how difficult and disruptive it is to daily life. Training the second implant meant giving myself near-constant daily headaches.

I'm fully adjusted to my original implant, so I have no pain, but the constant beeping and robotic noises of the new implant are really painful during the adjustment period. Even with the potential for more depth perception, I haven't been able to convince myself to train with it when I feel like I hear just fine as is.

As a toddler, I didn't exactly have anything pressing to do with my time, and the brain is more adaptable to the new robotic noises at that age. But at twelve, I played soccer, ran cross-country, and was trying to do well in my classes. I am a firm believer that parents know what is right for their children, and the executive decision she made for Rachel and me made our lives so much easier.

I wasn't sure how and when to decide to officially quit trying with the second implant though. Rachel had always had a different relationship with her hearing loss than me. Whereas I had a comfortable relationship with silence, she wanted to hear as much as she could as often as she could. So if anyone was going to want to keep the second cochlear implant, it was her.

But even she struggled with it. It was actually Rachel that went to my mom and expressed she didn't want to keep trying. My mom knew right then that the second cochlear implant was not going to work out. Rachel would go to great lengths to improve her hearing, so if she didn't want to continue, it made sense to let the second implant go. And I couldn't have agreed more. In instances like these, having a sister that shared my disability really came in handy. Because, as always, Rachel was willing to say what we both were thinking.

And I felt affirmed knowing Rachel struggled with it as much as I did. On some level, I worried that I was being too lazy with the implant, that I wasn't working hard enough. But my sister always worked hard, and that was all the validation I needed to let the second implant go.

By middle school, I'd really flourished in my language development, so I didn't feel like that specifically isolated me in any way, though I was reaching a point where I preferred to hide my disability whenever possible to better fit in.

I didn't *really* fit in though. When other girls my age were starting to show interest in makeup and boys, I was still content to keep up with my sports and schoolwork. Whenever I was invited to do something like go to the mall on the weekend, I'd decline so I could stay home with my family. Chitchat at the mall food court was already difficult to understand, but add in the fact that the chitchat would revolve around boys? No, thanks.

I never felt bullied by my peers, and I didn't struggle to make friends, but I was a late bloomer. And even if nobody would say it outright, subconsciously I struggled with feelings that I was a burden to other people.

A regular part of my life was missed conversations. I'd be in the classroom, another student would turn to me, and I'd hear the equivalent of, "Abigail, bleht too glow?"

"What?" I'd have to ask.

And inevitably the person talking to me would sigh and shake their head. "Never mind."

Every time I failed to understand something and the people around me had to repeat themselves, I was an annoyance. It wasn't easy to communicate with me, and I was conscious of that.

At home, I never had to be a burden. With my family, I'd always be understood. They knew my needs and what I struggled with. So it was hard for me to choose to hang out with my peers instead of my family. They weren't really going to understand me, not completely. Hanging out with my siblings and parents was the easier thing to do. And it really helped to have a sister who shared my condition, even if our personalities were drastically different.

Rachel never hesitated to ask for the accommodations she needed, but as I moved into my high school years, this was something I struggled with severely. It's funny how different two siblings can end up, even though they're raised by the same person and, in this instance, have the same disability. Mom tried to instill the same qualities in us, to fight for our own needs and ask for treatment that would afford us the same opportunities as our peers.

My sister took this to heart. As the oldest, she felt a sense of responsibility that I never had to shoulder. Rachel knew she had to be the trailblazer for the both of us. For most of the teachers at our school, and many of our peers, she would be the first person they'd meet with a cochlear implant. When Rachel got her cochlear implant, she was the youngest child in Oregon to have the procedure. So even at age two, she was already a trailblazer.

In my eyes, my big sister had it all figured out and had come into her own confidence more easily than I did. She would eagerly tell teachers and friends about her hearing loss, confident that it would aid her community in understanding her better. In reality, she simply had to figure everything out by virtue of being the first to introduce our high school community to the cochlear implant. She had to have these conversations before I even came into the classroom, which set the tone for what teachers could expect in terms of accommodations. Even if it was uncomfortable for her, Rachel never had the luxury of keeping quiet. If she did, the both of us would've been left behind.

There were accommodations that Rachel couldn't have gone without. It was very important for her to receive lecture captioning, where a live translator would repeat what the teacher had said by typing it out on a laptop that Rachel could read from. Rachel learned by listening to every word of the lecture material, so it was critical for her that she got the same information as everyone around her.

Conversely, I was deeply introverted and hated any kind of attention, let alone attention to my hearing loss. Asking for accommodations in the classroom meant a lot of unwarranted attention. It wasn't like I could simply mention my hearing loss once to my teacher and then blend into the background. If I was to use the frequency modulation (FM) captioning system with a live translator, I had to sit in the front row with a bulky laptop on my desk. At the beginning of class, my teacher would have to boot up the machine and wait for it to connect, which was often a lengthy process. It slowed down the entire class and forced eyes on me.

Without the captioning system, I was undoubtedly missing some of the information in the lecture, but I didn't care about that. In a way, having Rachel as the trailblazer made things easier for me. I didn't have to step up to explain my hearing loss, which I appreciated as a highly introverted person. But in another sense, it put me into a box.

People tend to get the idea that individuals with the same disability require the same accommodations. For those who are born able-bodied, it's easy to assume that the same condition looks the same on every person. But that isn't the way our bodies and minds operate. The same way you and your coworker can catch the same cold and have very different symptoms, disability is not one-size-fits-all.

What was vital for Rachel's education wasn't necessarily vital for me. She needed to get her lecture material in full, while I learned far easier by studying textbooks. It was so much more important to me to blend in with my peers. I didn't need to hear every word of a lecture when I was just going to go home and study the textbook anyway.

So I dealt with a lot of assumptions that what would work for Rachel would work for me. And it didn't come naturally to me to say otherwise.

At that time, school was just as important to me as it was to my sister. We just took very different approaches. Both of us were in the IB program, a program designated for advanced students that places them in higher-level classes, similar to an honors program. Rachel and I shared virtually all the same teachers, which made it even harder for me to assimilate or speak up for my own personal needs.

All the teachers knew who I was and that I was deaf. Unfortunately, not all of them were open to making the classroom accessible. One history teacher in particular, Mrs. Dunn, hated the FM captioning system and never hid her annoyance at having to use it. Again, this wasn't a tool I likely would have chosen to use for myself, even though it expanded what I could understand of her lectures. But since my sister had Mrs. Dunn as a teacher before me and needed the captioning system, that expectation was already set.

The captioning system wasn't the easiest for teachers to use, so there was some pushback. I had to have that large old-looking laptop in front of me. My teachers would wear a bulky headset, not unlike what you'd see a nineties pop star wear during a concert. That headset recorded what my teacher said, so it could be typed out onto my laptop by a live translator. Though the process might have been an inconvenience, it was a common accommodation for students with a variety of hearing-loss conditions. But this teacher in particular had deemed the inconvenience not worth her time.

My mother was well aware of how difficult Mrs. Dunn had been about accommodating my sister, which meant she was prepared to deal with a lot of communication mishaps with her. Though, like me, confrontation didn't come naturally to my mother. She had to fight her own tendency to keep the peace to make sure Rachel and I were being treated fairly in the classroom. We worked with an advocate, Diane, who would meet with my teachers to go over the accommodations I needed and make sure I was receiving everything I required to be successful.

But with Mrs. Dunn, it was always a battle, and an embarrassing one for me. When she was teaching Rachel, she tried to exhibit a lot of control over the system she had to use for my sister to receive her captions. A system was provided to her, but instead of using it, she went out of her way to buy her own. Yeah, for reasons I never understood, she actually used her own money to purchase a captioning system, even though the school gave her one. That alone wouldn't necessarily be a problem, but she argued with my sister about using it, doubting that this system was even necessary. In her eyes, she was able to talk to Rachel just fine when they spoke one-on-one. So if Rachel had a cochlear implant that gave her the ability to hear, why did she have to go through all this hassle as her teacher?

This isn't that uncommon of an assumption. So many people see a cochlear implant as a cure for hearing loss. It isn't because most people with implants are still hard of hearing. I may call my implant my ear, but it isn't actually one. I'll always be more limited in my hearing than able-bodied individuals.

Because of the tension between this teacher and Rachel, my

mother and Diane were even more prepared to push for me when I got to her class. *Would that make this teacher hate me though? Would she grade me harder because she deemed me difficult?* That was where my mind was focused, not on whether I got to use the FM captioning system, which I didn't like to begin with.

I'd sit in one of the front seats with the cumbersome laptop crowding my desk.

"I feel like a superstar right now," Mrs. Dunn once said sarcastically after putting on the headset. I wanted to disappear into the walls. Why did she have to bring so much attention to it?

Then she'd groan while we waited for the connection to boot up for the remote transcriptionist. It wasn't the most efficient system. The captions would lag by ten seconds, which made it confusing if I was focused on listening, and sometimes the person transcribing would mishear my teacher.

Her loud sighs would inform the entire class what a nuisance she believed the system to be. And she'd make up a lot of rules for me while using it, fearing that I would use the captioning system to help other students cheat, though what was being captioned was exactly the same as the notes other students were taking anyway. As someone who was always a model student, this was deeply insulting.

We didn't butt heads as much as she did with Rachel, but that was solely because I tried so hard to be unassuming. I was very much a people pleaser in my early high school years. One experience I believe is universal, whether you're able-bodied or dealing with a disability, is the awkward phase that is the transition into high school.

For most people, this is a time when you're trying to piece together who you are and where you fit in. We want to be liked by our peers, to have a sense of community, and I very much didn't. For a while, it was difficult for me to make friends, and I'd spend my evenings studying at home or watching a lot of television. It was hard to connect with other people when I couldn't chat with them in the hallway or the cafeteria. I'd come to be haunted by the words *never mind*. And any conversation where the setting was too loud meant that I could miss something, and my conversation partner would have to sigh and say those dreaded words. Then I'd stand there, reminded of what a burden it was to speak to me.

This situation with my history teacher only ostracized me further. No matter how diplomatic I was, I feared my peers would see me as the girl with hearing loss who annoyed my teachers. My cochlear implant was a point against me, even before anyone got the opportunity to get to know me.

Even if I wasn't born deaf, I believe I would still have had a softer disposition; it's an innate part of my personality. But being deaf certainly exacerbated my nature to please others.

Imagine that as soon as you meet another person, you have to wonder if having a conversation with you is a chore. You're often asking someone to repeat themselves, or missing their inflection and struggling to focus on the meaning behind their words. So often, people skip having conversations with you, so they don't have to repeat themselves. This was my reality.

It instilled the idea that my struggle was a difficulty to everyone around me, and that I was a difficult person. It had nothing to do with my personality, and instead it was a physical quality I could never escape. No matter what, I would always be at least somewhat of a burden.

That weighed on me, and by high school, I knew I didn't want my struggles to burden anyone else. Whatever frustrations came with my hearing loss, I wanted them to be mine and mine alone. So I overcompensated with passivity.

At one point, I was so bothered by a particularly heated email thread with Mrs. Dunn, Diane, and my mom, that I secretly emailed Mrs. Dunn and apologized for Diane and my mom's behavior. Diane and my mother weren't being mean to her. In fact, my mom was often bending over backward to speak kindly to this teacher, to appeal to her in a way that didn't result in conflict. All she wanted was for her daughters to be given the same opportunities as their hearing peers, which wasn't a big ask. But this teacher made conversation without conflict extremely difficult, if not impossible. When reading over these emails, I completely agreed with the reasonable requests that Diane and my mother were making. Still, I wanted to get on Mrs. Dunn's good side, and I didn't tell Diane or my mom about the apology.

"I'm so sorry about my mom and Diane. I'm not going to ask

for any accommodations. I'm really enjoying your class so far this semester."

It was a blatant lie, but I did not want to get a bad grade in this class. And I was doing my best to not be the deaf girl who needed special help. If someone made a joke about my hearing loss, I'd laugh along, whether it bothered me or not. Rachel, on the other hand, would stick up for either of us if someone was being rude.

It was hard for me to understand how she could do that. How had she found her way through the mess that was the social hierarchy of high school? I wanted so badly to belong. Rachel's experience was, of course, very different in that she had her own struggles inwardly that I was not privy to. Having to chart the course for the both of us could not have been easy. I'm sure this is a universal experience for even able-bodied siblings. The oldest child often appears wise and accomplished because they gained experience in charting their own path, even though that path means they have to break down uncomfortable barriers for younger siblings. That's always a messy process, and I bet my sister didn't feel as wise as she looked to me. Still, I saw her as far more put together than me, which only furthered my frustrations at not being able to fit in.

There was a glimmer of hope though, when I decided to take an ASL class. I knew the teacher for the class was Deaf and only communicated through written word and ASL. I believed that'd be the one classroom where I could be comfortable. Maybe I'd finally get some understanding about my experiences and could relate to my teacher.

It didn't take long for me to realize my hope was entirely misplaced. The ASL course was nothing like I expected. It was the first class I took that wasn't part of the IB program with advanced students. I was very sheltered prior to that course. Before that, I didn't know any students who would regularly skip class or who didn't take their academics seriously. It was my first introduction to another world of high school. And that alone wouldn't have been a problem, but it wasn't a very pleasant introduction.

My teacher, Mr. Pritchett, made no secret of the fact that he didn't approve of my cochlear implant. On the very first day of class, he announced that he was Deaf but would never get a cochlear implant, nor would anyone else in his family. That being Deaf was not something to be fixed, but a culture to be embraced.

Which is a beautiful belief system. To fully embrace who you are, to identify strongly with your culture, that is an honorable and valid choice. One that I would have been curious to learn more about had my teacher simply told me about his personal beliefs in an open and educational manner.

The way he expressed his views went beyond educational though. There was real resentment for the fact that I had a cochlear implant, even though it was a choice made for me at a very young age. It never made sense to me why he had so much bitterness toward a decision that was made before I could even speak. It was as though the fact that I'd chosen to "cure" a condition that he didn't see as a disability was a direct affront to him. Though, as I've mentioned, cochlear implants aren't quite a cure for deafness, as there are still significant difficulties with hearing.

There are so many valid criticisms from Deaf activists about how cochlear implants are represented publicly, like the fact that much of the world sees the cochlear implant as an instant fix for deafness. You've probably seen videos online titled "Deaf Person Hears for the First Time" and clicked to find a smiling child listening to their mother say, "I love you." Deaf activists claim, rightfully so, that a lot of these videos are misleading. They imply that people can immediately understand language after their surgery, and that they get to walk away from the procedure as a happy hearing individual, when the truth is that training for a cochlear implant can be grueling. A lot of Deaf activists want more accurate representation, so that the deeply personal decision to get a cochlear implant can be an informed one. And that is a belief I fully agree with. It's a big part of my decision to write this book.

So I don't want to in any way imply that getting a cochlear implant is the right decision for everyone. The choice to not have one makes sense for so many people, and I've never judged anyone for deciding a cochlear implant wasn't for them. At the same time, it was deeply isolating to feel judgment because I had one. I thought I was walking into a class that would be more accessible to me, and instead, I was singled out. I had to sit through multiple documentaries that were anti–cochlear implant, when my classmates could clearly see I had one. As someone who hates being in the spotlight, it was agonizing to feel so much negative attention forced on me.

It didn't help that my ASL teacher was loved by the rest of the students. He ran his class in a cool way, without ever speaking, and everyone admired it. He'd communicate by writing things down or lip-reading. So when he'd go on a rant about how he disliked cochlear implants, everyone seemed to agree with him. I was the villain, the person who had made the horrible decision to get a cochlear implant. And it wasn't even *my* decision!

He didn't have to like cochlear implants, but as a teacher, he should've seen how he was ostracizing me as a person. By being so vocally anti–cochlear implant, he was basically saying to the class that he was anti-*me*.

That class was the first I ever skipped. I wouldn't even leave the school; I'd just find another place to sit until that class period was over, but it was still very out of character for me. Up until that point, I'd been a fastidious rule follower. Again, that was part of my people-pleasing nature, to keep everyone around me happy so that I might fit in. But what was the point? I'd already figured out that I'd never fully assimilate into the hearing community, and now from this class, I felt that the Deaf community didn't want me either.

I was living in limbo, not truly part of the hearing or Deaf worlds, when all I wanted so desperately was to belong somewhere. It forced me to reevaluate my approach.

Being the perfect rule-following, straight-A student hadn't

gotten me far socially. Trying my best to please everyone around me had sucked me dry with nothing to show for it. It hadn't made my history teacher approve of me, and it certainly didn't garner any favor with my ASL teacher. My social circle at the time was still pretty dry, and I was tired of spending my weekends at home with only movies to entertain me.

I wanted to fit in somewhere. From the harshness of my teacher, I was confident that I wouldn't be accepted into the Deaf community. Which meant I had to become a part of the hearing one, even if it meant shunning all accommodations and doing everything in my power to appear exactly like everyone else.

I set out to do just that.

Chapter 6

Though I was a late bloomer, every teen eventually hits that phase where they lean away from their family unit and rely more on their social circle. For me, that came in my junior year of high school.

But it might've been a little more complicated for me than the average teen. Because prior to my junior year, being at home had been my sanctuary. Socializing and having to navigate my disability with friends was always work, and that didn't change once I shifted to spending more time with friends than my family. Which meant that the comfort that once came so easily as a reprieve from the difficulty of socializing wasn't a constant in my life anymore.

My family was always there for me, of course. But we butted heads more after I decided I didn't want to comply with their rules. Once I got my license and had more control over where

I went and what I did, I got the opportunity to make my own rules, or at least ignore theirs as much as possible.

It was in my junior year that I started dating my first boyfriend. Though I never took much interest in school events like dances and football games, one of my friends was nominated for homecoming court, so we all rallied around her. She was taking this guy Jake as her homecoming date. He was just a friend. She had no romantic interest in him. So Jake and I ended up spending a lot of time together during homecoming.

At one point, he clumsily spilled a drink on me. Totally embarrassed, he apologized profusely.

"It's fine, really. Not a big deal," I told him.

"But I spilled on your dress! I've got to make it up to you. Why don't you give me your number and we can go out sometime, my treat?"

I was completely head over heels. Shortly after homecoming, we made it official. It was your stereotypical high school puppy-love story. I may have been late to have an interest in boys, but once I became serious about him, I fell hard.

And man, was I serious. I thought for sure we were the real deal. That we'd go to the same college and eventually get married. Naive, I know, but who isn't at that age? I thought I'd found "the one," and I wanted to spend all my time with him.

For the most part, I did. Since I was able to drive, I was able to meet him at his house, about twenty minutes away, regularly. I'd go over to his house often because his parents were a lot more relaxed than mine. He didn't really have any rules. His parents treated him like an adult, and he already had his own job and was extremely independent.

He actually lived twenty-five minutes away from our school, so he had an entirely different set of friends closer to home he'd hang out with. They were really popular at their school, which I wasn't, so it felt like I was living two very different lives. But soon enough, his friends became my friends.

This was where my rebellious phase really came into play. Though neither my boyfriend nor his friends ever pressured me to go out with them, I had an interest in the parties they'd attend. Like most teens, I was forbidden to drink, but that didn't stop me from lying about where I was so I could party with my new friends. Not that I ever went off the rails or anything. My grades slipped a little, but I still got mostly As and Bs. I made sure to make it home before curfew, even if I was lying about where I'd been.

It was a necessary step in the process of finding myself. I think for most people, high school is the start of figuring out who you want to be. It's when you make the decision about where you're going to go to school, what your future career is going to be. You're forced to reflect on yourself a lot more deeply than you ever have before.

For me, that reflection included figuring out who I was in relation to my hearing loss. Even as a kid, I never wanted to be a burden because of my disability and kept it to myself. But I leaned into that mentality even harder when I hit my junior year.

I didn't want to be my disability. I wanted to be Abigail, who-ever that girl was. I was still figuring it out. But she was more than just her hearing loss. A lot of people with disabilities or illnesses can probably relate to the battle between your condition and who you are, and how much of your condition *is* who you are. And like me, many people may decide that on the road to becoming the person they want to be, they don't want to think of their dis-ability at all. Hanging out with my boyfriend's friend group was the easiest way for me to do that.

In my younger years, when I felt that my hearing loss was an obstacle to socializing, I used my schoolwork and time with family to feel the comfort with my condition I always craved. But now that I wanted to be out with friends and my boyfriend, I had to take another approach to comfort.

Though my friends never made a big deal of my hearing loss, and they were always kind to me whenever it was brought up, my high school friendships were largely superficial. They didn't compare to the kind of understanding I received at home. And if I wanted that level of understanding, it would've required me to be really open about my condition in a way that I didn't want to be.

So I took the opposite approach and decided I wasn't ever going to bring it up. If I didn't mention my disability and didn't ask for accommodations, I believed people would just see me as Abigail—and this was my new definition of comfort. Even with my boyfriend, who I thought I was going to spend my life with, I didn't bring up my hearing loss often. He knew about it, everyone did, but I tried to make it a nonfactor in our relationship. And for the most part, it was.

In a way, I lived a double life. Out with my friends, I was just Abigail, but then I'd have to come back home, where my hearing loss was a regular part of my life. On the surface, most of my arguments with my parents were about my lack of focus in school or the fact that I was going out behind their backs, the kind of fights most teens end up having with their parents. But underneath that, I think I was experiencing an undercurrent of discomfort. When I was home, there was no escaping my hearing loss. I was distancing myself from my family because, by doing so, I also distanced myself from my disability. And at the time, it felt freeing.

Looking back on it, I can see how this was ultimately toxic for me. While I was definitely having a lot of fun socializing as this carefree, accommodation-free Abigail, the connections I was making weren't real. My friendships were all superficial, lacking real connection or understanding of who I was. But I was too busy having fun to notice.

You'd think a loud party would be difficult with a cochlear implant, considering how much I struggle with depth of sound. But loud parties were actually where I became most comfortable. Yes, it was hard to hear, but it was hard to hear for everyone. So I never felt out of place. When people are drinking, they don't seem to mind or even notice when you ask them to repeat themselves. Nobody is annoyed if you didn't hear them. Drunk people have their own struggles with communication. For maybe the first time in my life, I got to let loose with strangers. And drinking calmed my social anxieties, allowing me to feel free talking to people. It was a huge shift for me. I was gaining confidence in myself day by day.

But that confidence was shattered the day I saw a tweet from my boyfriend's ex.

I'd often wait for him to finish band practice so we could go home together. His ex was in band too, and every day when she exited practice, she'd give me a death glare. I'd never done anything to her, but she definitely didn't like that Jake and I were together.

There was one afternoon in particular where I was standing outside the band room door when she walked out. She rolled her eyes and whispered to some friends. I couldn't hear what she said, but she and her friends laughed loudly in front of me. I had a sinking gut feeling, but I couldn't put my finger on why. Jake drove me home, and I tried to keep my worries to myself, but those judgmental giggles were echoing in my mind.

"Everything alright?" he asked me.

"Yeah, fine." I didn't want to bother him with this.

He dropped me off and I walked through my front door, set my backpack aside, and joined Stuart and Alistair on the couch where they were glued to some TV show I can't remember, probably because I wasn't able to focus on it. I just couldn't brush off that eye roll and decided to check her Twitter account, even though I doubted I'd find anything useful. It wasn't like she was going to tweet about laughing at me after band, right?

I scrolled through her last few tweets, and my heart dropped into my stomach.

Until that day, I'd never been bullied or harassed because of my hearing loss by any of my peers. Though I always internalized the feeling that I might be a burden, nobody had ever come right out and said it. But the tweet said exactly that.

"She thinks because she's deaf, she can get anything she wants."

Though I rarely ever cried, the tears came quick. I knew she didn't like me, but this seemed like such a low blow. My hearing loss had nothing to do with the fact that I was dating her ex.

I was on the couch with my brothers, who hadn't noticed that I'd started crying, but my mom did.

"Abigail, what is it?" she asked.

I showed her the tweet. Maybe I should've let the comment slide right off my back, chalked it up to a jealous ex-girlfriend. But that was easier said than done.

"Don't pay her any attention. She just wants to bother you."

As usual, Mom was right. And though I was really tempted to tweet back, I didn't. I didn't want to give her the attention she was craving.

But whether she knew it or not, she'd hit on my worst insecurity. She may have been jealous, but if this was how she perceived me, did others think the same thing? Was she just saying what everyone else was thinking? It didn't help that I found the tweet myself. It had been up for a day or two, but nobody brought it to my attention. I felt like nobody had my back, which only furthered my worries that everyone agreed with her.

The last thing I ever wanted to do was use my hearing loss to gain sympathy and special treatment. I was just trying to be like everyone else! Even asking for accommodations in the classroom had been difficult for me. I couldn't imagine trying to get other forms of preferential treatment.

I decided then and there I was never going to bring up my hearing loss. I wasn't going to talk about it. I certainly wasn't going to ask for help. If people thought I got special treatment due to my hearing loss, I'd go in the exact opposite direction and get no accommodations at all.

It wasn't a healthy mentality, but it was the only way I knew how to deal with the emotional damage of reading that tweet. Already I'd been pushing away my disability from my identity, but after that I pushed harder.

My boyfriend was planning on going to Oregon State University, as were several of our friends, so I made the same plan. My parents definitely didn't approve of me deciding where I wanted to go to college based on my boyfriend's choices, which in retrospect was fair. They saw that the more time I spent with him, the more my priorities shifted, and it's hard to blame them for being critical of our relationship.

At the time, I didn't see it that way. This was the man I was going to marry, so I hated that they didn't seem to like him or the idea of our relationship continuing into college. It created a bigger divide and more tension at home.

I didn't take my mom seriously when she said Oregon State probably wasn't a great choice because of my hearing loss. I'd already decided I wasn't going to let my hearing loss be a factor in where I went and believed I could handle a big school. In my mind, this was just another way my mother was trying to drive a wedge between my boyfriend and me.

In actuality, her concerns made a lot of sense. At a big school with large lecture halls, it was going to be significantly harder for me to understand what the professors were saying. My mom insisted she'd support my decision about going to Oregon State only if I agreed to attend one lecture there to find out if I could hear. I didn't do that, preferring to believe that she just didn't get it. I was going to be happy at Oregon State. I was sure of it.

For my parents, it was frustrating to watch me push away potential accommodations that would benefit me. It's a struggle so many parents who have a disabled child go through. In their eyes, I was denying myself a better education and a school that would better cater to my needs as someone with hearing loss. But my mom knew she had to give me the freedom to make these choices, even if it put me at a disadvantage. At the end of the day, it was more important for me to make autonomous decisions for myself. She couldn't hold my hand through my life. She had to let go and trust I'd be fine with the choices I made.

Rachel also pushed me to go to a small private school though.

She was attending Willamette University, which was just five minutes from my parents' house, and she loved it. It was a small school, and she thought the smaller class sizes were really helpful.

But Willamette was the exact opposite of what I wanted. There was no way I was going to attend a school just five minutes from my house. Isn't college supposed to be about breaking away, gaining freedom? The more autonomy I gained, the more I wanted. I was ready to get out of my small community and into the world.

Even more importantly, I'd spent eighteen years being Rachel's little sister. Everyone knew who I was and about my disability before I even got a chance to tell them. We'd always had the same teachers, and Rachel paved the way for what they expected of me. But being Rachel's little sister wasn't going to be my identity any more than my hearing loss was. I wanted to make my own friends, to be known on my own merit. At this point, Rachel and I still got along great. That was never the issue. I just didn't think I was going to be able to come into my own if I stayed in such close proximity to her. So, Oregon State seemed like the perfect solution.

Until my boyfriend broke up with me and started dating someone else.

It was October of my senior year, and we'd been dating for about a year at that point. But tensions were rising between us. He knew my parents didn't really like him. And I wasn't as much of a social butterfly as him, so often he held back on going out to chill with me. One day after school, we got into a small fight about how I'd been waiting on him to take me home, but he got caught up talking to some friends. It was such an unimportant thing, but sometimes little fights are representative of bigger problems.

"Yeah, Abigail, I don't think we're going to work out," he said, seemingly out of nowhere.

"What?"

"We just keep fighting. I don't think it's good for either of us."

I didn't even cry at the time. I was too stunned. It was that earth-shattering, end-of-the-world kind of breakup you expect from a first boyfriend.

I didn't want to go to school or my golf practices, which I usually loved. I didn't even care about college plans anymore. My life was over. Yes, it was very dramatic, but cut me a little slack for being seventeen.

And in my defense, the fallout in our social circle was pretty bad. It split the friend group down the middle, with the guys continuing to be his friends and the girls continuing to be mine. He was extremely charismatic, and though I'd become more social than I was in my younger years, I was still ultimately a subdued introvert. So, naturally, it was easier for the friend group to warm up to him again. Once he started bringing his new girlfriend around to the group hangouts, I no longer wanted to go. I ended up isolated.

In the end, it was for the best. Because I realized I didn't want to attend Oregon State after all. If college was supposed to be about me getting a fresh start, why would I go to the same school where all my old friends and boyfriend were going? It no longer made any sense to me.

Looking back, it's funny, because assimilating into this friend group was what pushed me to be independent. But in losing them, I fostered even more independence. I was finally making decisions for myself instead of basing them on what I thought my boyfriend wanted to do. As hard as it is to lose your first love, it's a uniquely grounding experience. For the first time, I realized happily ever after wasn't as easy as it looked, and my future wasn't going to be a straight shot from high school sweethearts to college education to married. I needed to learn that to figure out what my future was really going to be.

Ultimately, I decided on a small school, but not because I thought it would be a better fit. I chose Linfield University because they had a Division III golf program with an excellent coach. One of my biggest priorities was continuing to play golf through college, which had become a big passion of mine. They also had an excellent marketing program and, because of my experience with the Distributive Education Club of America, a business-focused club known as DECA, I thought marketing would be a good fit for me.

My mom was right though. The smaller school was a great fit for so many reasons. I'm so glad I chose Linfield over a larger school, because being in a small community allowed me to reach a new phase of acceptance with my hearing loss, one where I was able to integrate my identity as Abigail with my identity as a deaf person for the very first time.

Chapter 7

The summer before entering college, I had no plans to change how I was presenting myself publicly. I was still living with the mindset that I didn't want people seeing me as my disability, and I wanted to mention it as little as possible.

I was going to have to open up to my dorm roommate though. There was no getting around that. We'd be living together, so my hearing loss was going to become a facet of her daily life.

To say I was nervous to meet her would be an understatement. This was the person I'd spend my first year living with in college. It would've been nerve-racking no matter what, but knowing I'd have to introduce not just myself, but my hearing loss as well, was stressful. I couldn't keep up the same attitude I had with my old friends back home.

What kind of judgments might Elizabeth make once I told her about being deaf? The tweet still haunted me. Was I going to look like I wanted special treatment or attention? That had become one of my biggest fears, one I struggled to shake. But there was just no way to hide this if I was going to be living with someone.

We found each other on Facebook and decided to meet up before the semester started. She was already in our dorm early to train for the cross-country team. Elizabeth didn't have a car, so I picked her up. She wasn't hard to spot, because she was still in her cross-country outfit. I waved her over, and she waved back enthusiastically before hopping in my passenger seat with a smile and an extended hand. "So nice to finally meet you! You can call me Liz."

"Great to finally meet you too," I shook her hand. She didn't seem too nervous, so that put me at ease.

"Any idea where you want to grab lunch?" Liz asked.

"I don't know. I don't really know the area yet. I was hoping you did since you came early."

Liz bit her lip. "Actually, the only place I know of around here is Subway."

"Subway is good with me," I answered. I wasn't picky.

"Awesome!" Liz grinned. "Let's go!"

My first impression was that she was kind, confident, and potentially a great fit for me. But I still had to explain my condition and hope for a good reaction.

We each ordered a sandwich and took a seat at a table near the door. My anxiety was rising with every passing minute. I only got a few bites into my sandwich before the words came flying out my mouth.

"So I do need to tell you, I was born deaf. I actually have a cochlear implant that I wear in order to hear. But I might still struggle sometimes to understand you, and you'll probably find me in our dorm without my implant on pretty often, so I won't be able to hear you at all."

I was on the edge of my seat waiting for her response, looking for any sign of approval or rejection. She processed this for a moment, still in the middle of chewing. But every passing second felt like an eternity. Even if Liz didn't respond well, I'd be stuck with her for the rest of year, and I couldn't imagine spending a year with someone who judged me like Jacob's ex. But once she swallowed, to my relief, a smile crossed her face.

"Wait, so does this mean I don't have to worry about waking you up when I get ready for my morning cross-country practice?"

Needless to say, we were fast friends. I could not have been luckier with landing Liz as a roommate. Leaving home for the first time and living in an environment where not everyone would know and understand my disability was daunting. But Liz made that transition so much easier. From the very start, I had a friend on my side.

That didn't mean I was fully ready to open up to the rest of the world though. Keeping my disability to myself had worked for my friend group in high school, and for a while I believed I'd be able to manage the same thing in college. What I didn't realize was that college was a more intimate environment than high school had been, one that forces you to be honest about who you are.

I learned this lesson fast. During freshman orientation, my class of five hundred was sectioned into groups of twenty-five students, each scheduled for different activities. The first activity my group participated in was an icebreaker game to get to know each other. I scurried across campus, excited to meet some of my peers.

But as soon as I arrived, I heard a familiar *beep, beep, beep* in my ear. I knew what it meant. My battery was running low. In the chaos of getting settled into my dorm and my new routine on campus, I'd forgotten to bring a backup battery.

A swell of panic rose in my chest. I had a choice here, a difficult one. I could stay quiet, let my cochlear implant die, and try to fade into the background and hope nobody spoke to me. It wasn't too far off from what I had done so often in middle and high school. How many times had I been unable to hear what someone was saying and not asked for clarification? If I was careful, I may have been able to get out of this event without anyone really noticing me.

No, I didn't want to do that. For the first time in my life, I wanted to do things differently. I was here at college, coming into my own as an adult. I didn't want to fade into the background. With butterflies in my stomach, I raised my hand to speak up.

"Yes, is everything alright?" The orientation leader asked me.

"Actually, no. I'm deaf and need my cochlear implant to hear, but my battery is about to die. I'm going to need to run to my dorm room real quick. I can be back in ten minutes though."

All eyes were on me, the thing I most feared. In my head was a running list of my deepest insecurities. A little voice repeated the words, *She thinks because she's deaf she can get anything she wants.* I waited for the judgment to come, to see it in the faces of the people surrounding me.

But the judgment never came.

"Not a problem at all. You go right on ahead," the orientation leader told me.

And a flurry of smiles and nods in the group told me that nobody really minded. I grabbed my battery, returned to the orientation, and was treated with nothing but kindness from the group.

College forced me to restructure my relationship with my hearing loss. I wanted to be Abigail, just Abigail, but I couldn't be her if I didn't fully open up to those around me. And it was impossible to live with these people, share hallways and bathrooms with them, and not explain my condition. It went beyond just telling Liz. I couldn't have people thinking I was ignoring them every time I went to take a shower, just because I couldn't get my cochlear implant wet. If they were going to stop by our dorm to hang out, they needed to know that at times I wouldn't be able to hear them.

One of my new friends, Kasey, stopped by our dorm room a lot, and she quickly became a fixture in my life. We'd eat every meal together, get ready for every frat party in my dorm room. It didn't take long for this bond to far exceed the relationships I had in high school. Because for the first time, I was myself, completely, even while I was still figuring out who that person was.

It wasn't always easy, but I was rewarded time and time again for allowing my friends to know the real me. There was one time in particular when another new friend of mine, Molly, was hanging out with one of her basketball teammates, talking about their first impressions of people at the school. Her teammate Lisa started talking about this really rude girl in her dorm.

"Her name is Abigail. She's a snob; stay far away. I thought she was cool at first, but I was wrong."

Molly was stunned because she'd never had anything but nice experiences with me. "What did she do?"

"Well, I called out to her while I was walking to class, and she totally ignored me! Didn't give me the time of day. I don't know what I did to her."

Molly couldn't help but chuckle. "Lisa, Abigail is deaf. She wears a cochlear implant. She just didn't hear you."

We all had a laugh about this later. Had I not been so open about my condition early on, though, who knows how long people would've gone around believing me to be the campus snob. At such a small school, where there were only about 1,700 people, the last thing I wanted was for a big chunk of the campus to hear I wasn't friendly. It served as a reminder that the more honest I was about my disability, the better people could understand me.

Talking about my hearing loss didn't mean I wasn't going to be viewed as Abigail as I once feared. It meant that people would finally get to know me as I am.

Prior to college, the only people I was able to lean on fully were my family. In college, my friends became that family. I think that's a pretty universal experience for a lot of people, able-bodied or not. We all have to go through a period of finding our independence in early adulthood, and that often involves moving away from family. You have to find a home away from home, and that creates strong bonds, which, for me, have become lifelong.

Living in the dorms on my own was the first time I realized my friends could accept me just as deeply as my own family. I could be just as vulnerable, just as authentic, and they'd not only be willing to accommodate me, but eager to do so. I never felt like a burden to Liz, who was always quick to repeat something someone said if I didn't hear it, and introduced me as a friend who was hard of hearing so that whatever group of people we were hanging out with, I would be comfortable.

Though most of my class sizes were small, there was one lecture-hall-style psychology course that I was nervous about. I had a few friends who would be in the class, including Liz, and we all agreed to sit together. But I knew some of those friends would want to sit farther back, so it would be easier to chat or goof off without notice.

But sitting in the back of a class was a huge detriment to me in a room with sixty other students. I had to be close to the teacher, but I didn't want to be the one to speak up and ask to sit in the front row. Thankfully, I didn't have to be.

We all walked in, and I scanned the large room, trying to figure out how difficult it would be for me to hear in the back row. I knew right away that I'd barely be able to hear. It was a large class, with rows and rows of seating. At the very back, the professor's voice would echo, and I wouldn't be able to make out a word.

I think my concern read on my face, because when Liz turned to me, her face contorted slightly.

"Guys, can we sit closer to the professor? I want to make sure I'm not missing anything," Liz asked.

I knew straight off what she was doing and tried to keep my little smile to myself. I may have been learning to advocate for myself more and more in college, but it was great when I didn't have to. My friends were looking out for me, something I'd never experienced before in my life. Prior to college, my family were my only advocates. And let's be real, my family *has* to support me. They're my family. I can expect them to support me more than other people because I can never be a burden to them, and so often I still felt like one to everyone else.

Through my friends, I was able to accept that I wasn't a burden, though it still took me a little while to realize that.

During rush week, Kasey and I got invited to a toga party by some guys who were rushing Theta Chi. We spent the day shopping for toga materials, then went back to my dorm to wrap the sheets around ourselves and create cute leaf headbands.

We were so excited that in the midst of the pregame chaos, I forgot to change my battery. (Forgetting to change out my battery wasn't exactly a rare occurrence for me at college, if that wasn't obvious.) I was so disappointed with myself. We'd nearly reached the party after spending so much time getting ready, and my dorm was a fifteen-minute walk away. I was determined to not make it Kasey's problem though.

"I'm so sorry, but my battery is dying on my implant."

Kasey looked at me. "Do we need to go back?"

We. The word came out of her mouth so effortlessly, like it wasn't even a question. But I wanted it to be clear that she was under no obligation to go with me.

"I'm just going to go run and get it. I won't be too long."

"You're not going alone! It's totally fine. I'll go with you," Kasey insisted.

I was never alone at Linfield. My friends were so deeply accommodating that I finally stopped worrying about how my hearing loss would affect my social life. They saw me entirely as I was and wanted to support me however they could.

Slowly, this unconditional acceptance transformed my life. I developed a confidence in myself that I'd never had before. I was able to start joking about my hearing loss, something I'd never been able to do before. If I wanted people to be comfortable around me though, I didn't want to seem like I took my disability too seriously. If I missed something someone said, I'd joke about it, and we'd all be able to laugh at my misunderstandings instead of sitting there awkwardly any time I needed a sentence repeated. I was never the butt of any joke. Nobody ever made fun of my hearing loss, but it became a lighthearted topic rather than the elephant in the room.

In those college years, so much of my personality had shifted for the better. Along with that came more changes, including my major, marketing. Though I thought I'd love marketing from my time in DECA, I realized the job was very communal. There were a lot of meetings with large groups of people, and projects were often worked on in groups. Even if I didn't have hearing loss, as I'm a bit of an introvert, I preferred to have a job where I was working primarily on my own. But combined with how much I struggled to hear in a group setting, marketing began to feel like the wrong fit.

My junior year I took a finance class that made me reconsider marketing entirely. I enjoyed focusing on numbers. I was one of only three other girls in the class. The men in the class were a lot more vocal than me. I tended to keep my head down and do my assignments. But Professor Romero wasn't having it. One day, she asked to speak with me after class.

Immediately, my mind went to the worst possible scenario. Had I done something wrong? That didn't add up. I had a great grade in the class, and it's not like I ever interrupted.

"Is everything alright?" I asked, nervous.

Professor Romero cleared her throat and pushed back her blond hair. She always looked so put together. "Abigail, you're doing a wonderful job. I can see you really understand the material."

"Okay, great..." I was waiting for the *but*.

"But if I could offer any advice, it would be to speak up a little more. I wish you'd put some of these guys in their place!"

I laughed. "Okay, I'll try."

"What's your major?" she asked.

"Marketing."

Professor Romero, who clearly didn't share my problem of struggling to speak her mind, shook her head. "No, that's not right. You need to be in finance. You're perfect for it, and I can tell you're enjoying it."

She was right. I was already unsure if marketing was the right choice for me. But I needed that nudge to go in a different direction. So, with her support, I changed majors.

And Professor Romero continued to support me through my senior year. She had a connection with a company in Portland that typically hired five or six undergrads a year, and she was able to get me a position there. So, my senior year of college, it seemed like everything was lining up well for me. There were very few fears I had about the future, because it seemed everything was falling into place.

If there was anything I worried about after graduation, it was that I'd miss college. My years at Linfield were transformative for me. I loved my friends. I loved the life I built. But I knew I'd take the lessons and friendships with me wherever I went.

So, after graduation, I took the job Professor Romero lined up. Kasey also got a job in Portland, and we decided to get an apartment together. A new phase of my life was beginning, and I felt prepared to take it on.

But my transition from college to adult life wasn't as smooth as I would've hoped.

Chapter 8

Like most twenty-two-year-olds, I believed I had a solid plan for my life. After graduation, I got an apartment with Kasey right outside Portland, the city where we both worked. Now that I had my degree, I was fully prepared to enter the workforce, take my dating life more seriously, find the guy I was supposed to settle down with, and begin my new adult life.

But even before graduation, this new phase in my life was off to a rocky start. My grandfather, who had been born with a congenital heart defect, was in heart failure, so sick that he could barely attend my graduation and had to be in a wheelchair.

He'd had a heart attack many years before but began to deteriorate during my senior year at Linfield. He lost a lot of weight and became scarily pale and thin. Doctors warned him that his heart was failing, and without a transplant, he would not make it. There was a point where we believed he only had months left, and I was spending as much time with my grandparents as I could. Grandpa was determined to get a transplant though.

"I've got to get a transplant, otherwise I won't be able to see you and your sister get married," he told me.

"Grandpa, why are you thinking about that right now? I'm nowhere near getting married!" I answered.

Mom nudged him. "Yeah, don't put that idea in their heads. It's way too soon!"

We all joked about it, but the seriousness of the situation was clear. Still, I was hopeful he'd be okay.

He wasn't eligible for a heart transplant in Oregon due to his age, so my grandparents moved to Los Angeles near a hospital where his age wouldn't be a factor. Other than his heart, he was incredibly healthy, and the fall after my graduation he got the call that a heart was available.

He'd had the surgery a few days before my arrival in LA to visit him, so by the time I got there, he was already acting like everything was fine. Grandpa hated asking for help, especially in a medical setting. They say doctors make the worst patients, and my grandpa is a clear example of that. But I was so happy he was improving. With his health on the rise, I was able to focus on my plans for the future.

At that time, I was hopeful about what my future held. Growing up, I'd always been told that if I went to college and got a degree in a practical field, I'd make decent money and would enjoy my job. But like a lot of people my age, my experience didn't line up with the dream. Despite getting a highly coveted job, I was working long hours for little money.

The confidence I'd found in college faded somewhat in the workplace. Sure, I'd found a way to talk about my hearing loss among my university friends, but announcing my condition at my job was far more difficult. It wasn't a place where I could easily joke around—a tool I'd used when explaining my hearing loss to others in the past. And like so many disabled people, I had a lot of fear that announcing my disability during an interview would keep me from getting the job. So, I lay low, choosing not to explain my cochlear implant.

That got me into a few sticky situations though.

We frequently had group meetings, which were already hard for me to follow. In one particular meeting, my boss took his seat, fiddled with his tie a bit, then turned to me.

"Abigail, would you mind taking notes?"

I actually did mind, but because I didn't yet know how to navigate my disability in the workplace, what came out of my mouth was, "Sure."

The meetings were fast-paced, with pieces of conversation occasionally overlapping each other. It always takes me a second to process what I'm hearing, and I was rushing to get that information on paper while also struggling to process the next overlapping topic. I was absolutely missing vital bits of information when taking notes.

But like so many disabled people in the workplace, I didn't

want to seem like I wasn't fully capable of doing my job. And though asking for accommodations definitely didn't mean I wasn't doing my job, that's what it often felt like. So once again, I was back in the position of not getting my needs met.

Regardless of my struggles in the workplace, there was still an excitement that came with living in Portland on my own. I was ready to start dating after staying single for most of college. After my dramatic high school heartbreak, I became a little cold in dating, choosing to keep my relationships casual. But that mindset changed once I moved to Portland. Most of my friends, including Kasey, were in relationships and weren't able to go out with me every weekend like we'd done in college. I saw them lean into their serious relationships for companionship, and I wanted that too.

Still, I was ready to live my best *Sex and the City* life, hoping that, because I was in a big city now, I'd meet tons of different guys and date around until I met the one who would sweep me off my feet.

I learned quickly there's probably a reason that *Sex and the City* was set in New York instead of Portland, Oregon. Needless to say, my dating life wasn't any more fulfilling than my work life. A lot of the time, I would end up messaging a guy for a while but would never plan any actual dates. Dating is uncomfortable for everyone, but it's notably difficult for me (*especially* in a city full of trendy restaurants with loud music and crowds of chattering people).

I never spoke up about my preferred location for dates

though. When a guy suggested we go somewhere, I went along with it, because I wanted to seem like a cool girl, a trap I think many women fall into in their early twenties. I had this idea that to appear desirable to men, I needed to seem flexible, laid-back. When we'd chat over dating apps, I'd never mention my hearing loss, because I didn't want to seem like a girl who needed to make a big deal of her disability. In my head, I'd play out a fantasy where a guy just happened to notice my cochlear implant on a first date, and I'd mention it casually. They'd see how chill I was, and we'd be on to date two, followed by many more dates.

The reality was that I rarely ever got a date two, because on date one I'd appear completely aloof. It was hard to hear, I often missed crucial pieces of conversation, and the men I was going out with didn't understand why I occasionally ignored them. On my mission to be a cool girl, I ended up looking like a snob.

Looking back, I think it would've looked a lot cooler if I was up-front about my hearing loss from the beginning. I'm sure most of the guys I went on dates with would've respected the honesty and seen it as a green flag for further dates, on top of understanding that I wasn't ignoring them on purpose. And honesty would've led to a more open, intimate connection. But nobody wants to engage in intimate conversation if they think you're disregarding them.

I'll never forget a particularly awful date with this guy Dave, who really impressed me when he saw on my profile that I golfed and invited me to Top Golf for a little friendly competition. Not only did he plan the date himself, but he made the choice based on *my* interests. And he was pretty cute, so I was excited to see where it'd lead.

At first, things were going really well. He met me outside Top Golf and was just as good-looking in person as he had been in his profile. The chemistry between us was strong, and I was sure it would continue for the rest of the date.

Things changed once we got out to the bay though. Suddenly, it was so much louder. There were people yelling and laughing all around us.

I went up to swing, and Dave sat on my right side. The problem was I could only hear from my left. Every once in a while, I'd catch a stray word from him, but not enough to understand what he was saying. I'd laugh or nod along; then I'd watch his face contort. We were absolutely not communicating, and I left the date hoping for a second one that would never happen.

But failed dates weren't a big deal because, at the time, dating was one big game I was playing. I'd plan my moves and keep my real feelings close to my chest. It was a way to protect my own heart and stay one step ahead of the men I was seeing. Though it wasn't conducive to fostering a real connection.

Eventually, I put dating on hold to spend more time with my family. After my grandpa's transplant surgery, my grandparents were able to move back to Oregon, and the family was able to spend a lot more time together. I visited often, relieved to see how much Grandpa had improved. We were able to spend the holidays with one another, and a few days before Christmas, we went to see a biopic on Winston Churchill, which Granny really liked.

During our Christmas celebration, we decided to play a game of Heads Up. It's a game where you hold a card up to your forehead and your team has to try and get you to guess the word without saying it. It was Granny's turn, and she put the word *ladder* on her forehead.

"You need this to put up Christmas lights," I called out.

Granny hesitated to answer, which was a bit weird because she was usually pretty quick with her answers.

"You climb up it to reach high places," Alistair continued to explain.

"Oh, a ladder," Granny laughed as the timer went off. For a moment, we all laughed along with her.

Until her next words came out of her mouth.

"Winston, it's your turn!" Granny said to my dad.

We all looked around at each other. Mom's eyebrows had fallen, a bit of concern on her face. "Did you just say Winston, Granny?" I asked.

"Weston!" she corrected herself. "I guess I was still thinking about the movie."

It seemed like an innocent enough slipup, so we brushed it off.

Until other odd incidents began to pop up. One day, Granny showed up at my parents' house, ready to go for a walk they'd planned. Except my mom hadn't planned any walk with Granny. It wasn't a huge red flag. Granny was older, and it didn't seem too concerning that she might get her plans mixed up. There was no harm in getting a checkup though, just to make sure nothing was wrong.

A few weeks later, I was on my way home after work when my phone rang. It was my mom. Which was weird because, although we chatted on the phone regularly, my mom usually sent a text first to see if I had time to talk. It's such a small gesture, but the absence of it had alarm bells ringing in my head. I picked up quickly, hopeful that I'd just missed the text somehow.

"Hello?"

"Abigail, we need to talk." My mom's voice was already cracking.

I can probably count on one hand the amount of times I've heard my mom cry. She isn't an emotional woman, having inherited her mother's Scottish stoicism. But she couldn't hold back her emotions that day. My first clue that something was terribly wrong.

"I went to the doctor today with Granny. They told us that Granny has stage four glioblastoma. I don't have a lot more information yet, but it's very serious. She's going to have to undergo brain surgery very soon."

I couldn't respond. Not just because the information had collapsed in on me like a toppling building (which it had), but because I knew I wouldn't be able to speak without crying. And like my mother, I didn't cry often. If my mom knew tears were filling my eyes, she'd break down too. She was trying to keep it together. I could feel that even over the phone, and I wouldn't be the one to push her over the edge.

"I love you. Will you and Rachel come down this weekend?"

This, at least, I could answer without hesitation. "Yes, of course. We'll be there."

We drove down the next day, and every weekend after that. After that call, I still held onto a bit of hope that Granny would pull through. I mean, just a few months ago, we believed it would be Grandpa's last Christmas, and that ended up alright. I hadn't yet experienced a tragedy that didn't have a happy ending, and so I held on to the naivete that comes with youth, the kind of naivete that insists you and your loved ones are invincible. You'll all live forever, even if you intellectually know that isn't true. You can't emotionally grasp loss until you've felt it.

None of us expected that it would be Granny, not Grandpa, who spent her last Christmas with us that year. After her surgery, it became clear just how bleak the situation was. The tumor was not resectable, and the glioblastoma, an aggressive cancer, would continue to grow rapidly.

It all happened so fast. Just weeks before, we were all planning her birthday. My uncle was going to fly into town, and the whole family was going to visit a local winery. Instead, we were all gathering at her bedside in the hospital.

Still, Granny wouldn't allow any negativity. Even as we all stood around her hospital bed, she wanted to talk about how wonderful it was that we were all together.

"It's so great to be able to spend time with you guys," she said as casually as if we really were all spending a day at the winery.

The room was decorated with flowers and birthday balloons, but that didn't change the ambiance for me. She grabbed my hands and clapped them together with hers, something she'd done all my life when she was excited. I just couldn't keep up that excitement with her.

It felt weird to try and be as happy as she appeared to be. I mean, it was her birthday, and she was spending it in a hospital. It all felt so wrong to me, and that must have shown on my face, because when I sat down in a chair next to my mom, she leaned over and whispered to me, "Granny just wants to keep things light. She doesn't want to talk about the surgery or the tumor."

My last image of her before surgery was of her smiling face. It was the last time I saw her smile.

After surgery, Granny took a drastic turn for the worse. She couldn't speak to us and instead would look around the room aimlessly. Immediately, she was taken home under hospice care, where she was placed in the living room, overlooking the golf course that neighbored her house. Where the television once was, we placed Granny's medical bed. We didn't need a TV. When we came over, it was just to see Granny. The couch and chairs all faced her. None of us wanted to look at anything else.

Though she couldn't speak to us, Rachel and I came down every weekend to see her. My parents and brothers were also frequent visitors, taking every opportunity they could to talk to Granny and tell her about the latest family news.

"Abigail just got promoted at work. We are so proud of her." Mom would beam at Granny, who could only stare at the window.

We'd have coffee and lunch, keeping my Grandpa company. He was still looking healthy after his surgery, even if his heart was stricken by grief. It was a cruel twist of fate that he believed he'd be the one needing Granny's care, and just a few months after his transplant, he was now caring for her in her last moments.

It was amazing to witness the love Grandpa had for my Granny. After their many years of marriage, he was deeply dedicated to her. She was in her worst moments, not even able to speak, and never did he turn away from her. It's the kind of love you see in books and movies, the kind I believed in when I was a hopelessly romantic teen. And on some level, I think I stopped believing in it after my first heartbreak, choosing to treat relationships like a chess game where I always had to make the next right move to keep a man intrigued.

My Granny couldn't play chess; she couldn't even move. And to her very last breath, my Grandpa loved her completely, unendingly.

Though we all knew it was coming, her death was not easy on anyone. My family leaned on each other after her funeral, spending time together, both laughing and crying at old memories. Our bonds grew stronger, even as grief made us weak.

I tried to spend as much time with my family as I could after

Granny's death. Rachel and I would drive into Salem, and we'd all have lunch at my parents' house. It was a regular occurrence for us. So I didn't know what to expect when, at one particular lunch, Grandpa said he had a gift for us.

"A gift?" I asked. It wasn't a holiday, wasn't my birthday. I didn't usually get random gifts from Grandpa.

He handed me a small, thin square package. Carefully, I peeled back the edges of the gift wrap to reveal a bright red book with Granny's photo on the cover.

In his grief, Grandpa made a book about Granny's life, sharing all the things we didn't know about her. Granny never talked about her life too much. She was prideful and private. But Grandpa wanted to make sure we all knew about the amazing life she lived. All the kids got a copy of the book, which included pictures of all of us together.

I spent hours and hours that afternoon flipping through those pages. I learned so much about her that I didn't realize I didn't know. Stories from her childhood, their wedding day, the sacrifices it took to come to America with my Grandpa. As sad as it was to know she wasn't with me any longer, the book gave me a little bit of closure. She had lived such a happy, full life. I keep that book in my nightstand to this day.

Though I'd always been immeasurably close to my grandparents, it was during this grieving period that I really got to see how much my Granny did for me, through stories from my parents. I can't remember the time period when my biological dad left. I only recall the wonderful moments I had coloring in the living room of the apartment my grandparents rented so we could all live together. As an adult, I finally understood what it meant for my grandparents to uproot their life not once, but multiple times in order to be there for me and my siblings. It's hard to picture how my mom could have gotten two toddlers through two different cochlear implant surgeries alone. Financially and emotionally, my granny was there every step of the way.

My world shifted after Granny's death, and it felt like I had lived two lives. There was all the time I had with her, and the time I had after her. I wasn't the same person after grieving her. I don't think anyone ever is after their first loss. Whether that happens when you're very young or much older, it's a universal experience, having a loved one pass. And you don't really know that experience until it happens. It can't be explained, can't be prepared for. The only certainty is that when it happens, you will never be the same.

The version of Abigail before Granny passed had a seemingly endless amount of time on her hands. She was just twenty-three, the rest of her life waiting for her. She hadn't decided what to prioritize in her life, because why would she? There is an invincibility you feel when you're young. It takes watching someone you love die to face your own mortality. My granny may have been much older than me, but suddenly twenty-three didn't feel so young. Because now my life had a timeline; it would end. And the people I loved, their lives would end too. Time isn't to be wasted but cherished. There is a finite amount of it that we all get. And I wanted to spend my time happy, grateful, and at peace with my choices.

I definitely didn't have peace before we got Granny's diagnosis. I wasn't happy with my job, my dating life; I was dealing with a consistent state of loneliness. The only reason I didn't do anything about it is because I'd grown so complacent in my life, but that changed. With my new promotion, I felt a newfound freedom to discuss my hearing loss and the accommodations I needed, like wanting to be kept off projects where I'd have to make a lot of client calls or take meeting notes. But even with the pay raise, I was dissatisfied with my position. So I left.

The changes in my life began to happen rapidly. I moved in with Rachel, took a job in Vancouver, the same city where we once lived with my grandparents. I would be working at a real estate company with a small finance department. I only worked with five other people but believed that would be a better fit for my needs.

I would've given anything to still have my granny by my side, but I carried her with me as much as I could. She guided my decisions. I knew she would've wanted me to be my most authentic self, to live larger than life, to build my own happiness. And with that guidance, I finally was creating a life I believed I'd be really happy with. Slowly, I was settling into this new reality without her and was so deeply appreciative of all the little things I used to take for granted.

But I couldn't predict that a big curveball was about to come my way. Things were about to shift yet again, not just for me, but for the entire world. The pandemic changed everyone's life, there's no denying that. So many people got put into lockdown, stuck at home with not much to do but watch television. And somehow, I ended up on their TVs.

Chapter 9

Though I had high hopes initially that my new job in Vancouver would be the right fit for me, I realized fast it wasn't where I was supposed to be. Often, I felt bored, and I was still at a place in my life where I wanted to take risks. Life was too short to stay at a job where I wouldn't be happy.

So when I came across an ad for an event planning company looking for someone in the budgeting department, I went for it. On paper, it might not have seemed like the perfect fit. Event planning meant a lot more phone calls and direct interaction with clients. But I was starting to doubt whether finance was the right path for me. The solitary nature of the job made working with my hearing loss easier, but I wanted to socialize more. The event planning job seemed perfect since I'd be working with numbers, but I could dip my toes into another field and see how I liked it.

For the first time, I was fully transparent about my hearing loss from the very first interview. This was before Zoom was popular, so there was no phone or video interview. Which, personally, I really loved because talking in person is way easier for me.

I drove to Beaverton to the company's office. As soon as I walked in the door, I was put at ease. It was a trendy office, the walls colorfully decorated with photos of past events. All the meeting rooms had glass cubicles and already I could see people collaborating at large conference tables.

The interviewing managers, Elliot and Lauren, were only a few years older than me, so the environment was much more casual. I felt like I was talking to my peers. That made it a little easier to bring up my hearing loss. And it definitely needed to be brought up. I knew my hearing loss might directly impact my performance in this position, so I wasn't going to beat around the bush.

"So, a lot of the job is talking to the clients over the phone or video calls. You'll be setting up those meetings. How comfortable are you on the phone?" Elliot asked me.

"Very comfortable. But I do want to be fully transparent that I use a cochlear implant. I do just fine on phone and video calls, but one thing I've learned from my past jobs is that I'm not the best person to take notes in a meeting. It might be better to delegate that task to someone else."

"Thank you so much for sharing that," Lauren answered with a smile. "We definitely don't want you to feel obligated to do that. There are plenty of other people who can take meeting notes."

They were both very accommodating, and after one more interview, I was offered the position.

It seemed like life was really falling into place for me. It had been over a year since Granny passed, and though I miss her to this day, I was settling into life without her. I'd finally reached a level of confidence with my hearing loss that allowed me to be myself not just in social situations, but in the workplace too. I was living with my sister in Beaverton right outside of Portland, and I loved having her as a part of my daily life. We'd often exercise together after work or watch a show together when our free time lined up. Though dating was still a bit of a nightmare, I had an amazing group of girlfriends who were all single too. We all had office jobs and were living for the weekend. Every Saturday, we'd get dressed up to go to have dinner and barhop.

I still treasure that time in my life. There is something really special about being in your early twenties and having a close group of friends you see every week. The older I get, the more hectic my life becomes, and I don't have that same core group of friends. I get to meet a lot of people now, which is a blast, but it was a weight off my shoulders to have close friends that knew me deeply. They knew about my hearing loss and were steadfast supporters. I loved the relationships I had with them and the rhythm that had formed in my weekly routine.

Until COVID-19 came along.

When I first applied to the event planning job, there were rumblings of a virus spreading in China, but it didn't concern me.

The media often sensationalize bad news, so it's hard to know when something is an actual threat. I pushed the news out of my mind and continued living my life.

I had weekend plans for my birthday, which was the first week in March. I was going to get dressed up and go to a couple of bars with my girlfriends. Honestly, I didn't have any concerns about it. But a few of my friends were hesitant.

"I don't know if we should be going out this weekend. Everyone keeps talking about this coronavirus," one of my girlfriends texted me.

I brushed it off. "I mean, I don't get sick that easily. It's kind of like the flu, right? I haven't gotten the flu in ages."

I wasn't terribly concerned and went out as planned. A lot of other people in the city went barhopping that weekend too, which reinforced the idea that this was one big overblown media circus. But the following Monday, I got the call that my office had been shut down, along with all nonessential businesses in Portland.

For the first time, I realized the gravity of the situation.

I'd only been working for two weeks, so switching to working from home was a huge transition for me. But still, with the news repeating phrases like, "Two weeks to flatten the curve," I was hopeful I'd be back in the office soon enough.

Then the layoffs began. Even though I was a recent hire, I wasn't fired right away, because the budget team still had work to do. Sure, new events were not currently being planned, but part of my job was to go over budget reports from past events.

Weeks went by, and anyone whose job was directly related to planning new events was let go. But I kept my head down and focused on my work. The first month of lockdown wasn't too stressful for me. I'd been getting a little burned out by constantly going out every weekend, so I took this time to recharge.

I had my sister when I wanted someone to chat with, but a lot of my time was spent doing home workouts, taking long showers, and cooking elaborate meals that I usually didn't have time for. When we needed fresh air, Rachel would suggest we go for a long walk. I treated it like an extended period of self-care, and because I was sure this was a short-term adjustment, I enjoyed it.

But a month turned into two, and soon even the budget team no longer had any new work. I was furloughed in June, and with no end to the pandemic in sight, the stress hit me. What was I going to do if my job didn't ask me to come back? That seemed the most likely situation. And it wasn't like there were places hiring, since most people had just been let go from their jobs.

I was able to collect unemployment, but I had begun to really panic. On top of losing my job, I was going stir-crazy without my friends. Once it was clear that outdoor activities were Covid safe, my friend Molly wanted to meet at a lake in Washington to spend the weekend together.

As excited as I was to see her, the worries about my job continued to stress me out. I'd been obsessively checking websites for job ads, even though I knew I was unlikely to find anything.

Still, while I was laying out on a towel by the water, I browsed ads. One piqued my interest.

"Oh my god, look what I just found." I flashed the phone to Molly, showing her an ad looking for *Bachelor* contestants.

I'd been a *Bachelor* fan ever since I walked in on my mom watching Sean Lowe's season. It was a silly reality TV show, but Mom and I really enjoyed watching it together. My social media feeds were flooded with information about the "quarantine crew" of this season of *The Bachelor*, and Matt James was revealed to be the newest Bachelor on *Good Morning America*. At the time, my friends and I joked about how hot he was. Of course, I never pictured myself on *The Bachelor*. I was just excited because Matt was definitely going to be fun to watch next season.

"You absolutely have to apply!" Molly nudged me.

I laughed. "You're crazy. I'm not going to go on *The Bachelor*!"

"I know! But just for fun. See what they say. Maybe you'll learn some behind-the-scenes stuff."

I was positive I wouldn't get far enough in the process to share any juicy *Bachelor* details. But as a joke, I went ahead and applied. All they really wanted was my name, some pictures, and a short bio.

"So what should my bio be? That I'm single and unlucky in love?" It was corny, but honest.

"No! You're not going to stand out that way. You'll go right in the pile of rejections. Say something interesting about yourself."

I thought about this for a moment. "I don't think I've ever seen anyone with a cochlear implant on the show."

"That's perfect!"

I wrote about how I was deaf and looking for love, then sent off the application. I had no expectations that I'd hear back, but at least we had a good time joking about it during our lake hangout.

I told Rachel, my mom, and some other friends that I'd applied as a joke. Everyone was hopeful I'd at least get a call back so I could tell them all about it, but I was confident that wouldn't be happening.

The tap house underneath our apartment had opened up some outdoor seating, so Rachel and I decided to go have a drink there the following week. I was sipping a beer, talking to Rachel about the concerns I had about finding a new job, when my phone started ringing. It was an unknown number from California.

"It must be *The Bachelor*!" I showed Rachel the phone, though I still wasn't entirely sure who was calling.

"Pick up! You've got to find out!"

I hesitated, having no clue what I'd say if it actually was a call from *The Bachelor*. But with every ring, I knew I was running out of time, so I quickly picked up.

"Hello?"

"Hi, I'm calling for Abigail Heringer."

"This is she."

"Abigail, hello. I'm calling about your application for *The Bachelor*. We think you might be a great fit for the next season. Would you be available for a Zoom call next week?"

To say I was stunned would be an understatement. I agreed to the call, then immediately told all my friends about my call-back. Of course, I still had no intention of actually going on *The Bachelor*. But at least I'd get all the juicy details about the casting process my friends were looking for.

And we had a lot of fun with it. After my introductory Zoom call, they requested that I record a video talking about different aspects of my life. My girlfriends Nohea, Kasey, Molly, and Liz came over with a few bottles of wine. We drank while we picked out my outfit and planned my video. They helped me come up with ideas for how I could stand out.

The Bachelor casting became a small bright spot during a very boring time in my life. It gave us all something to joke and gossip about. Every time I did a new interview or sent them a video, I expected the rejection call to come. And for the most part, I think all my friends were expecting the same. The idea that I'd actually make it on *The Bachelor* was too far-fetched.

I'd seen enough of *The Bachelor* to know I didn't have the type of personality they were looking for. I wasn't loud. I didn't have the kind of temperament that would cause a lot of drama. It was obvious from my interviews that I had a more subdued nature, and I was sure they would see that I'd keep to myself if I actually was cast. It was just a matter of waiting for them to put a stop to the interview process once they saw I wasn't a good fit.

The possibility that they might actually want me on the show was in the back of my mind, of course. But I already knew that if they asked me, I'd decline. What was I going to do on a reality TV show? Sure, I'd had a hard time dating, but I hardly thought *The Bachelor* was going to be the answer to that problem. If I struggled to go on normal dates, what was I going to do with thirty-one other women competing to date the same guy? On top of that, I had never been one to be the center of attention, so the idea of being on national television was terrifying.

I didn't even bother telling my mom that I was still being interviewed. I didn't think she'd approve, and it didn't matter because I wasn't going to be on the show.

A few weeks passed with no more news. I'd headed over to my friend Jennah's place to have a drink and a sleepover. As they often do, one drink turned into one too many. The next morning, I woke up on her couch with a massive headache. I hadn't remembered to charge my phone, so it was dead on the coffee table. But I grabbed it, plugged it into the charger, and realized I had multiple missed calls that morning, all of them from California. I didn't see any voicemails, but saw I had a new email from the casting crew. Surely, it would be about my rejection.

I gasped when I opened it to read the exact opposite.

"What is it?" Jennah turned to me, concerned.

"They want me to come out to film for *The Bachelor*."

"No way!" Jennah squealed.

But I couldn't share her excitement. All the thrills I'd felt during this process disappeared. This wasn't fun anymore. It was serious. They actually wanted me to fly out and be on *The Bachelor*. I was in a state of denial as the stress rushed over me. They needed an answer by tomorrow.

What was I going to tell them? I had to say no, of course. Would they be upset that I'd wasted their time with this process? The anxiety was getting to me.

I called my mom, though I'd left her out of the loop on this whole process. I fully expected that once I told her about the opportunity, she'd immediately shut it down. No way was she going to want to see me on a reality television show, and I was inclined to agree with her. I think a part of me called her specifically so she *would* make it known that it was a horrible idea, and I could tell the producers I wouldn't be going, confident it was the right decision because Mom agreed with me.

But I never could have predicted Mom's reaction.

"So don't be mad, but you know how I applied for *The Bachelor*?"

"Yes, why?" Mom asked, her tone tentative.

"Because the process may have been a little more serious than I let on. They actually just emailed me, and they want me on the show."

Quiet for a moment on the other line. I waited for her disapproval.

"Wow. Is that something you want to do?"

"I mean, it's crazy, right? But then again, it is an opportunity not a lot of people get offered. I'm torn."

"Do they know about your hearing loss?" she asked.

"Yes. I told them on my first application."

"And would you be comfortable talking about that on the show? Because they're definitely going to ask you to talk about it."

"Yeah, I think so."

This was it. The moment when she would shut the idea down and tell me how difficult it was going to be to talk about my disability on national television. And she was probably right. Was I really ready to be that vulnerable?

"This could be a great opportunity, Abigail."

What?

"They've never had a contestant with a cochlear implant before. As long as you stay true to yourself, and don't do anything that you think would reflect badly on your character, it could be a chance to teach people about hearing loss."

I called my mom hoping she was going to talk me out of going on the show, but she'd done the exact opposite. Up until that point, I hadn't even considered the impact I might make for other people with hearing loss and cochlear implants.

As soon as I realized what a difference I could make, my mind was made up. I was absolutely going to go on *The Bachelor*. It would be a wild ride, but I let myself get excited about meeting Matt. I'd done my research, and he seemed smart, handsome, and kind. The exact kind of guy I should be dating.

But what was it going to be like to date him alongside thirty-one other women?

Chapter 10

Making the decision to go on *The Bachelor* was the hard part, but preparing to go on the show wasn't exactly a walk in the park either. There was a lot of planning I needed to do.

The producers gave me a list of clothes I'd need to bring, including at least seven dresses. At the time, I only owned three. The Portland bar scene was pretty casual, so I didn't have much of a need to buy new dresses. I was on a pretty tight budget since I'd been furloughed. And if that wasn't stressful enough, most of the shops in Portland were still closed due to Covid. The only places I could go dress shopping in person were Macy's and JCPenney, but those dresses were better suited for homecoming than a rose ceremony.

I had to turn to online shopping, which was stressful since I couldn't try things on, and I had a limited amount of time to get my wardrobe together. I didn't spend more than a hundred bucks on a dress, but even bargain-hunted outfits were out of my budget. To make matters worse, I was pretty confident I wouldn't make it past the first week or two—if I even got a rose on the first night. I was likely spending hundreds of dollars I didn't have on dresses I wouldn't even wear.

Then it hit me. If I wasn't going to wear the dresses, there was no reason I couldn't return them. I wasn't proud of this plan, but I could keep the tags on the dresses and make sure I shipped them back when I got home. There was a thirty-day return window on most of the clothes I bought, and I'd surely be back within thirty days. (The joke was on me. I wasn't able to return a single one of those dresses.)

But that was my plan, and I felt a little better about spending the money knowing I'd get it all back next month. In addition to the dresses, I had to pack a lot of warm clothes, jackets, and boots. And all of this had to fit into just two suitcases. If you noticed I was a major outfit repeater on the show, you have to cut me some slack. It's nearly impossible to fit several weeks' worth of outfits into just two suitcases.

On top of all the clothes, I had to make sure I was packing every essential. Normally while traveling, I'm somewhat relaxed about making sure I have things like nail clippers or a hairbrush. I can always run to a local drugstore to pick up anything I forget. But on *The Bachelor*, I would be in a bubble. There would be nowhere to shop, no place to go. The hotel might have had some shampoo and soap, but mostly, I would be on my own.

I was able to stop by Macy's one evening with my mom. My parents wanted to help out and get me a few dresses. While walking through the store, we passed the luggage section, and Mom stopped me.

"Abigail, what suitcases were you planning to bring?"

I hadn't really thought about this. "My usual ones, I guess."

We had family suitcases that had been passed down over the course of many years, some of them from before I was even born. They looked as ratty as you might expect, with random stains and frayed edges.

"You cannot bring those suitcases on the show. When they send women home, they usually show someone coming to collect their bags. No way are you putting those suitcases on national television."

I'd completely forgotten about that. We grabbed two cute new suitcases. I didn't know it at the time, but before one-on-one dates, the producers ask the women to pack up their luggage just in case they get sent home. But I ended up going home on a group date, and I don't think anyone expected I'd be going home that night, least of all me. So my suitcases never made it on national television. But I assure you, they were adorable.

By the time I'd shopped for most of my outfits, I still hadn't found a dress I loved enough to wear on the first night. The first night of *The Bachelor* could be my only night, so I wanted to look my best. But I had no idea where to begin looking for a nice evening gown. This would be the nicest dress I'd ever bought. The only dress that even came close was for prom. I texted one of the producers and asked if they had any suggestions about where I should look for a dress.

"Honestly, I'd try bridal shops. Ask to look at bridesmaid dresses."

Okay, this was going to be a little weird. I'd never even been close to getting proposed to, and I figured the first time I'd shop in a bridal boutique would be for my own wedding. But it was a good idea, so Mom and Dad tagged along to look for my night-one dress.

We went to a local boutique, and it was basically empty. A very attentive employee walked over to us right away.

"What can I help you with today?"

"I'm looking for an evening gown, actually. Something floor-length, though I don't really have a style in mind," I told her.

She wore the typical ear-to-ear customer service smile. "Absolutely! And what is the gown for?"

I froze. First rule of *The Bachelor*, don't tell anyone about *The Bachelor*. I was under strict orders not to talk about the show. Obviously, I bent those rules a bit for my family, but I certainly couldn't tell a random bridal boutique employee.

Mom covered for me, though she's not a much better liar than I am. Her answer was super vague. "Oh, she's got a big event coming up."

Immediately, this garnered a confused look from the employee, and I couldn't figure out why at first. Then it hit me. Of course, with Covid, what big event would I be attending? No wonder the bridal shop was empty. They got hit just as hard by Covid as the event planning business.

Thankfully, though, the bridal shop employee didn't ask any more questions. My parents ended up buying the most expensive dress in my collection, and I was ready to wrap up all my shopping. Sooner than later, I'd be on a plane headed to Pennsylvania.

Mom and Rachel took me to the airport, and I was instructed to film some B-roll videos while I waited for my flight. Never had I filmed myself talking to my phone in a public place, so that was extremely awkward. I had my mom and Rachel sit in front of me so I could huddle in a corner and film myself without being seen. I basically recorded myself saying how excited I was to meet Matt. It never made it onto the show, probably because I looked as awkward on the video as I felt!

I was thrilled to finally get on the plane, so I had an excuse to put my phone away. Though the mask wasn't the most comfortable, it was at the point in the pandemic when the middle seats were being left open on all flights, which was amazing. I had more legroom than I'd ever had on a plane before.

Excitement was bubbling out of me after I landed. I found someone who had my name written down on a placard, and they took me to my car.

Before the show began, I'd be staying in a hotel room prior to production, but I didn't much mind this. A hotel stay actually sounded kind of nice. I imagined myself soaking in a hot tub, pampering myself with hotel amenities.

My imagination didn't account for the fact that I wouldn't be leaving my room.

A staff member led me through the hotel halls, then opened the door to a dark lodge room with minimal natural lighting. I walked in, they closed the door behind me, and that was the last time I saw anyone until the production began.

I didn't even see the person who dropped off my meals. They'd set the food down, knock on the door, and would be gone before I got there. At least for the first few days, I was allowed to have my phone. I spent a lot of the time binging Netflix.

But *Bachelor* rules meant that after those first few days, they took my phone, and I was left with just the hotel television. Which would've been fine, except the TV didn't have closed captioning. For obvious reasons, I'm the kind of person who needs captioning on every show and movie I watch. I miss bits and pieces of conversation if I can't read the captions. I should've brought some books with me, but I didn't exactly have extra room in my suitcase.

I filled some of the time by practicing makeup looks and trying on my dresses. I still hadn't decided what I'd be wearing the first night. The dress my parents bought from the bridal boutique was a sparkly pink gown, but sparkles didn't feel like my style. Instead, I settled on a dark blue dress, not because I liked it the most, but because it was the easiest to walk in. I knew I'd be walking up a few flights of stairs after meeting Matt, and I was terrified to fall flat on my face. Heels weren't something I wore regularly, so I practiced walking around my room.

I think for most people, being in a hotel room is an uncomfortable environment, but I felt especially vulnerable with my hearing loss. Normally, to go to sleep, I take my ear off and drift off to complete silence.

But removing my cochlear implant meant not being able to hear anything, and I knew at any time a producer or staff member could knock on my door. And what if there was an emergency? Sure, the producers knew I was deaf, but would that be their first thought if the building had to be evacuated? I had to look out for myself, which meant keeping my ear on at all times.

I can't fully express how draining it is to wear my implant all hours of the day. I could barely sleep. From what I understand, most hearing individuals are able to filter out small noises while they rest. But since I have to put in effort to process what I hear, every tiny noise would spark a series of questions for me. *What was that? What direction did that noise come from?* I couldn't just hear a noise and not think about what I was hearing. With these questions swirling around my head over every minor noise, restorative sleep was hard to come by.

A few days before production began, things got a little more exciting. I was asked to do a photo shoot for promotional pictures. It only took an hour, but it was nice to get out of my room for a bit. And the producers began to prep me on what to expect for night one. We wouldn't start filming until the sun went down, so I was told to sleep in as long as possible.

When the day finally arrived, I got up around 2:00 p.m. I had my lunch, then started to get ready. Of course, I finished getting dressed way too soon, and had to sit and wait for someone to come get me.

I expected that I'd have some sort of anxiety before meeting Matt, but the hotel stay had made me so stir-crazy that I was only excited. I desperately wanted out of my room. If anything, I was more nervous to meet the other girls than Matt.

Past seasons of *The Bachelor* taught me that ladies can get catty on the show. My plan was to keep to myself and stay out of the drama. The last thing I wanted was to get into a reality television fight.

But when someone came to take me to the limo, I was pleasantly surprised by how nice the other girls were. I sat between Marylynn and Magi, and we all hit it off right away. They were so sweet, and nobody even brought up Matt. Instead, we complimented each other's outfits.

"Are you excited?" Magi asked, a smile plastered on her face.

Talking to the two of them, it was impossible not to notice how stunningly gorgeous they were. Up until that point, I hadn't seen any of the other women. I knew they'd be gorgeous, but it seemed like I was surrounded by actual supermodels. Suddenly, I felt incredibly out of place. What was I doing here? Was I seriously about to get out of this limo and meet Matt on national television?

"Would anyone like a glass of champagne?" the limousine attendant asked.

Everyone else declined, but my hand shot up. "I'll take one." I absolutely needed a drink to calm my nerves.

I distracted myself by repeating my opening line in my head. Some girls planned really extravagant openers, some even included props, but I couldn't bring myself to do that. I didn't have a naturally over-the-top personality. At first, I considered using my cochlear implant battery as a prop. I would hand it to Matt and tell him how I'd be needing it later, so he should come find me, but then I thought better of that. Probably best not to give him something so vital. I didn't want him to feel bad for losing it, and I knew he was going to be handed a lot of props.

We pulled up to the entrance of Nemacolin, and suddenly, I was in an enchanted Disney fairy tale. I'd never seen a building quite so extravagant. I knew I'd be walking up a few flights of stairs, but this was more than a few flights. The staircase to the doorway seemed to go on forever.

The girls all squealed when we saw Matt standing there. He was as handsome in person as he'd been in his photos online. I shared in the excitement, eagerly waving out the window at Matt, which was corny, but I didn't care because the windows were tinted.

My heart nearly dropped into my stomach when Matt waved back. Okay, so they weren't tinted, and I had just made myself look like an absolute goofball. No matter, I had to shake it off.

Soon I'd exit the limo and introduce myself. Now I was definitely nervous to meet Matt. I'd already made a silly mistake, but it would be the last goofy thing I did that night. I promised myself that.

But I broke that promise just a few minutes later when I got out of the limo and somehow closed the door on my own hip. Since I wasn't light on my feet in heels, I stumbled back, and Matt couldn't contain his laughter. Not my most gracious moment, but at least we could laugh about it.

Being out of the limo, I was acutely aware that we were being watched. Was I really doing this? It was hard to take it all in, but I focused on Matt, blocking out everything else.

After seeing Matt plastered all over social media as the newest Bachelor, it was easy to see him as this larger-than-life personality. But as I stepped closer, I could see that he was just as nervous as I was. That was such a great comfort, and I reminded myself that this was his first time on the show too. We'd be going through this journey for the first time together. Knowing this, I was able to talk with him a little easier.

"Hi, how are you?" He smiled at me, and I couldn't help but melt a bit. He was really good-looking, and hearing his laughter a moment ago was disarming.

As much as he was analyzing me, I was analyzing him too. It's easy for people to forget that it isn't just the Bachelor who's evaluating which contestants would be a good fit. The women on the show also needed to figure out if Matt could fit into their lives.

Personally, I wanted a guy I could talk with easily, someone who could make me laugh. So far, Matt was off to a good start.

I had planned out what I wanted to say, but now that I was standing in front of Matt, I nearly forgot every word. Bright lights were shining on my face, and I didn't expect them to be so hot. My hands were shaking. I can barely remember the words that came from my mouth next.

"So there is something a little bit different about me, and that is I'm deaf. So I'm going to be reading your lips a lot tonight. But thankfully, you have really beautiful lips, so I'm not complaining."

Matt laughed and held both my hands. "I love that. I'm going to enunciate for you."

I told him how I was eager to speak with him more, but as I walked away, it was hard to know if I'd really made an impression on him. Maybe that would be the only conversation I got to have with him that night.

I'd soon find out I made a lot more of an impression than I thought.

Chapter 11

The steps up to Nemacolin may as well have been a mountain. I had two minutes to talk to Matt and then had to spend five minutes just walking up the stairs. When I imagined myself on a reality TV show, I expected everything to move fast, because that was the pacing of *The Bachelor* whenever I watched it. Instead, time moved more slowly, because I knew all eyes would be on me until the next girl went to greet Matt. My walk up to the cocktail party was the longest five minutes of my life.

But time only seemed to move more slowly once I actually entered Nemacolin. There were already about twenty other girls mingling who had come in before me. I wasn't sure where to go or what to do, so I made my way to the bar. There were a few other women grabbing drinks, so I didn't feel too out of place. Like me, I think they needed a little liquid courage to get through the night.

I searched the room for a familiar face and found Marylynn

from my limo ride. She was sitting with another group of girls, who were all happily chatting about what they had done for their intro. Everyone was friendly, yet I still felt a tension in the air. Not because of Matt and the competition for him, but because I was acutely aware that anything I did would end up on national television. Intellectually, I knew I was going to be on a TV show, but knowing it and actually living it are two different things. I scrutinized my every move. Was I sitting the right way? Talking too much? Too little?

"So, what did you do for your intro?" Magi asked after she made her way to Marylynn and me.

I hadn't told anyone in the limo about my implant. There was just so much going on. It didn't fit into the conversation naturally.

"Well, I have hearing loss and use a cochlear implant. So I told Matt I'd be reading his lips a lot tonight but teased him about having great lips to look at."

This garnered a few chuckles from the surrounding women. Nobody questioned my disability or made a huge deal about it. It was hardly a big talking point, considering how the introductions became stranger and stranger as the night went on. I mean, who wants to chat about my cochlear implant after watching Katie introduce herself with a vibrator?

Watching more women enter, it all became so surreal. When Queen Victoria came into the room, I had to ask myself, was this even real? Everyone was using gimmicks on the show, but it created an environment unlike anything you'd see in the real world.

It wouldn't be until later that I realized, despite all the gimmicks, we were all just normal women thrust into a strange environment.

But standing out was never my strong suit. Once all the women had arrived and we were asked to squeeze in on the living room couch, I realized just how easily I blended in. What was going to make Matt notice me instead of all these other women?

We were all jammed together on the couch when Chris Harrison walked out to introduce Matt. Immediately, I was star-struck. Up until that point, I'd never met a celebrity, and I'd been watching this man on TV for years. As much as I tried to play it cool, I was fangirling hard.

Chris welcomed us. "How are we feeling tonight, ladies?"

Honestly, I was feeling like this night wasn't real. I'd seen him on TV so many times, but to hear his voice right in front of me was bizarre.

"The journey of love begins now. Remember, it's important to stand out tonight, because a lot of women will unfortunately be going home."

It was hard not to wonder if that would be me. I half expected it would be but tried to keep an open heart and open mind.

When Matt finally came out, I still sensed a bit of nervousness in him. "Oh, man. I had so long to think about what I'm going to say to you all. But I think I'm going to do something different."

He led us in a prayer, which really endeared him to me. He seemed authentic, and though we'd only spent a few minutes together, my interest in him was piqued.

On paper, he checked off so many boxes. Dating in Portland, I'd meet guy after guy, and none of them stood out like Matt. He was handsome and laid-back, had a secure job, and could make me laugh. There was still so much to learn about him, but that was part of the appeal for me. The other Bachelors had appeared on TV already, and their lives were well-documented on social media and in gossip magazines. But not Matt. Matt was a mystery, and I wanted to learn more.

But after his introduction, everyone wanted to talk to him, of course. Time with him was a hot commodity, and not every woman got that time.

It was such a strange situation to be placed in, to be one of thirty-two women who all wanted the same guy. But in a way, I think that pressure increased my attraction to Matt. With so many other women fawning over him, I started to feel like I'd just met the hottest man in the entire country. I was just as eager to talk to him as everyone else.

So many of the women around me were stressed about whether they'd get any time with Matt at all. The later it got, the more tension there was at the cocktail party. It was nearly two in the morning when I finally got a chance to talk to him. I had to interrupt Jessenia to get a minute with him, which was intensely awkward for me. The last thing I wanted was for my first conversation with Matt to begin with an interruption. But Jessenia was sweet about it, as the girls usually were. We all knew this was the name of the game, and were understanding when another girl came to have her time with Matt. Still, I felt an awkwardness when I sat down next to him.

But any tension was quickly relieved when he greeted me. "Abigail, so nice to see you."

So he had remembered me. I had already made an impression. That put me at ease. But it was still so hard to know what to talk about. It had to be overwhelming for him to have thirty-two different conversations over the course of the night. Some of those conversations would be forgettable small talk, and others would be really intense conversations involving personal history and trauma. I liked to take things slow when dating, not revealing too much about myself at first. But that didn't seem effective for making connections on *The Bachelor*.

At least it was the perfect dating setup for me. I so often struggled with going out to dinner on a first date due to how hard it was to hear in a busy restaurant. But since the set had to be quiet while filming, that meant it was easy to hear and understand Matt. We got to talking about our families. Being close to family was one thing we had in common. I shared about how I'd always been close to my grandparents, parents, and siblings.

"Your sister, Rachel, was also born deaf? What was that like?" he asked.

I filled him in on some of the details of our childhood and the process of getting a cochlear implant. The conversation was surprisingly easy. For the first time since my arrival, I wasn't focused on the fact that I was on a reality television show. Nobody was in that room but us, and the moment felt so natural. Nothing about it was manufactured. And I was stunned by how comfortable it all was.

"I'm really glad you're here," Matt said softly.

"And I'm really glad you're the Bachelor."

And then it happened. He leaned in and kissed me. He had me stunned speechless. What had just happened? Was I really kissing the Bachelor right now? Every woman at Nemacolin wanted this man, but here he was, kissing me. It was impossible not to feel a twinge of excitement. Mom was going to kill me. She made me promise not to make her fly out for hometowns, which was usually the portion of the show when the Bachelor would fly out to see the hometown and visit the family of the women he was still courting. Due to Covid, it would be done backward this season, with the family flying out to the set of the show to meet. I insisted I wasn't going to be on the show that long. But after that kiss, I wasn't so sure!

But I tried to rein in those feelings. Sure, he might have been kissing me, but how many other women had he kissed? It would be foolish to assume I was the only one.

Still, we clearly had a connection. It was shocking how much I liked Matt after just a five-minute conversation. I was usually the one to take things very slow. I'd dated guys for months back home without the situationship ever shifting into a real relationship. But if I'd met Matt on a normal date, I probably would've gone home and told my girlfriends I'd just found my husband.

Things between us felt so easy, and I could see a real relationship growing.

This wasn't a normal date though. And there were more than thirty other women there who were probably having intimate moments with him. It wasn't just me. I had to remember that. I figured I was one of many women Matt had kissed that night. I had to slow my roll.

I reminded myself after our conversation was done, and I went back to the cocktail party. The other women were sharing bits and pieces of the conversations they had with Matt. Most of them were as starry-eyed as me. After hearing how hopeful some of the other women were, I had no expectation that I was going to get the first impression rose. I had to just be satisfied that we shared a great moment, even if it was one of many Matt had that night.

It was five in the morning when Chris Harrison came out to set down the first impression rose. I was sitting on a couch next to Queen Victoria with an espresso martini in hand, fighting to stay awake. I'd slept until 2:00 p.m. but was now wishing I'd slept even later than that. But the thrill of knowing someone was about to get the first impression rose woke me up a bit, and I sat up a little straighter as Matt walked in.

The women were scattered in different areas, and Matt walked in a big circle, looping around the room. He walked up to the couch where I was seated, and my heart was nearly beating out of my chest. Would he give me the first impression rose?

No. He passed me and continued to loop around the room. *Oh well.* I didn't let myself get too disappointed. What were the chances he was going to offer me the first rose?

He kept walking around the room, and I kept a close eye to see who he'd give the rose to. But he kept walking, and walking, and walking...

Matt had looped around the whole room and, once again, was at the couch in front of me. Finally, he stopped and stared down at me.

"Abigail, can we talk for a minute?" he asked.

"Sure," I answered, my eyes glued to the rose.

He didn't pick it up.

When he didn't take the rose, anxiety got the best of me. I'd watched the show, so I knew that women were sometimes sent home on the spot because the Bachelor wasn't feeling a connection. If he wanted to talk to me, but didn't want to give me the rose, I had to mentally prepare to pack my bags.

We sat down together on the same couch where we shared our first kiss. There was no smile on my face because it took all my energy not to show my concern. Nobody wanted to go home on the very first night, especially considering all the time and money it took to get to the show. If I spent all that time in a hotel waiting to see Matt just to get driven back to the airport, I'd be more than a little disappointed.

"I had a great time with you tonight," Matt began. "It took a lot of strength to share your story."

I was waiting for the *but*. *But I don't feel a connection with you. But I'm not sure this is the best environment for you.* I was so sure the next words out of his mouth were going to send me home.

Matt paused. Here came the rejection.

"Can you give me just a minute?" he asked.

What?

He left the room. Was he having second thoughts about sending me home? Why was he delaying this? I could've jumped out of my skin with nervousness. But I waited patiently for him to return.

When he did, he held one hand behind his back.

I'd read this all wrong. He wasn't sending me home! I was getting the first impression rose. Now I was smiling so hard, it hurt my cheeks a little.

He revealed the rose. "The one thing I asked of the women tonight was to be vulnerable. Knowing that you're a fighter, I think it's only appropriate I ask you something. Abigail, will you accept this rose?"

"I will!" The words came out immediately.

I was living in a fantasy. All the women he could have given his first impression rose to, and he chose me. So the instant connection I felt was mutual.

I no longer had to worry about the rose ceremony. I was safe. And even better, if I was Matt's first connection here, it gave me so much hope for our time on *The Bachelor*. Could Matt really be the man I ended up with? After all my dating failures, what were the chances that *The Bachelor* led me to the person I was supposed to be with? I had so much hope for the coming weeks.

But that hope would be dashed when I realized how limited that time really was. I thought our instant connection would lead to us growing closer. Instead, that immediate attraction created distance between us.

Chapter 12

I was on a high walking into Falling Rock where all the women would be staying. Not only did I get the first impression rose, but I was stunned with my new living quarters.

The place was massive. Falling Rock was once a hotel, except the lobby had been changed to a hangout area for the women, with a large couch where we could all gather to receive date cards. They had a bar where we could order drinks at any time. Through the back windows, there was a gorgeous view of the golf course, and all the hotel rooms had a relaxing cabin vibe.

Normally on *The Bachelor*, women share large rooms and sleep in bunk beds. But because of Covid, the sleeping situation had to be changed. Instead, we would be staying in rooms paired with one other woman. Which felt like a nicer setup because it allowed for some privacy at night. And it was way more convenient, because I only had one roommate that I had to explain my hearing situation to.

If I had to live in the old *Bachelor*-style rooms, I would've had to explain to the whole group that I took my cochlear implant out at night and couldn't hear them, or remind them that in an emergency I need to be woken up by touch. It's harder to get dozens of people to learn my disability and accommodate it. But there was a comfort in having just one roommate to support me, like I did in college with Liz.

Shortly after our arrival, we all sat down on the large couch. Chris Harrison came out to greet us. Once again, I was fangirling, and I could tell some of the other women were too. The excitement of being on a reality television show was settling in. Here was Chris Harrison, likely ready to hand out a date card. The adventure was beginning.

"So, ladies, how did you all feel about meeting Matt?"

A lot of the women were open books, sharing their feelings and conversations they had with Matt. And normally I would be one too. Back home, I loved to spill to my girlfriends after I went on a date. Having such a tight-knit group of friends, it was really natural for me to want to share my dating experiences with the other women.

Except we were all dating the same guy, and I was the one who got the first impression rose. I'm not even the least bit confrontational. I could walk into a hair salon and ask for a trim, get six inches chopped off, and I'm still going to pretend to love it and leave a big tip. So the idea that some of these women might already have a problem with me because of the first impression rose was overwhelming.

I was keeping details of my night close to the chest. Secretly, I hoped Chris Harrison wouldn't direct the conversation toward me. He kept asking other women questions about Matt, and at first I thought I was off the hook.

But I should've known better. I got the first impression rose, so of course the conversation was eventually steered toward me.

"Abigail." When Chris said my name, my heart skipped a beat. "You got the first impression rose. Did you share a kiss with Matt?"

Well, he sure wasn't beating around the bush.

I froze. I've never been a good liar. "Yes," I blurted out truthfully, "just a quick peck."

I figured it would be better to be honest. The last thing I wanted was for any of the women in the house to think I was shady. Not to mention the fact that eventually the show would air, and everyone would know I kissed Matt.

Still, saying this definitely had me on edge. But it wasn't a big deal, right? I calmed myself with the thought that plenty of other women likely got kissed last night. Nobody was going to care.

But the room was silent. All eyes were on me. Most of the girls' faces had dropped, as had my stomach.

"Abigail." Chris Harrison looked directly at me. "You were the only girl last night that Matt kissed."

A mix of anxiety and joy hit me. I wish I'd known that before-hand. Maybe I would've tried to hide it. I didn't love the way everyone else in the room was looking at me.

But on the other hand, this was evidence that the connection I felt with Matt wasn't just in my head. He felt it too. I was the only woman he had kissed. And we kissed not just once, but twice! There was a real spark between us.

When Chris Harrison held out the date card, I hoped my name would be on it. I did my best to contain the butterflies as I waited at the edge of my seat.

"Bri," Chris Harrison read out.

Okay, well, it was probably unlikely that I'd get the first impression rose and the first date card. That made sense. And Matt was probably feeling pretty confident about our connection, so he didn't have to jump right into a one-on-one date.

Still, I wished so badly I could just pick up the phone and shoot him a text. If this was the real world, I would've already organized our next date. It was so weird to have such an instant connection without being able to explore it.

But that was part of the experience. I was sure we'd get our time soon enough.

I roomed with Magi, who was a blessing during my time on *The Bachelor*. Magi ended up being the perfect roommate. We had a small sidewalk area where we were allowed to walk, and Magi and I would go back and forth on the stretch of sidewalk daily and talk about our lives.

Magi had such a practical approach to being on *The Bachelor*. She was definitely interested in Matt, but she didn't let herself get too caught up in the process.

"If Matt isn't interested in me, then he's not the right fit," she told me. "I'm not going to chase him."

It was a really positive, relaxed attitude amidst a very intense process.

I wished I could emulate this, but like a lot of the other women, I found myself getting caught up in my emotions pretty quickly. Normally, I'd downplay my emotions while dating, so I never got my hopes up. The last thing I expected was that I'd get caught in my feelings during the show. But here I was, fully acknowledging my growing feelings for Matt and my desire to get to know him better.

But back home, I was able to go on a date and then go about my life. Go to work, hang out with my sister, chat with my girlfriends. I had other things going on. On *The Bachelor*, I had nothing outside of Matt to focus on.

Most of the conversations with the other women were centered around Matt.

"How strong do you think your connection with Matt is?"

"Do you think she has a stronger connection than you?"

"What do you think Matt is doing on his date right now?"

The questions were endless. Every day, we had to wait for a date card and hoped to get more time with him. All the activities and challenges on group dates were centered around Matt. The artificial pressure surrounding Matt led to very real feelings. All the other women wanted him, and so did I.

But I realized during the first group date that it was going to be hard for me to stand out in this environment.

It was a rainy day, so we all walked up with umbrellas in hand to find Matt standing in front of a photographer. He was dressed up in a suit, but I still didn't quite get what the date was about.

Matt welcomed us, then explained the plan for the day. "I'm confident that I can see my potential wife in this group. That said, I'm a visual person, and I thought it would be fun to have a little photo shoot and visualize what that special day would look like."

That's when I got a glimpse of the building behind him, all filled with wedding dresses.

Oh, no. As if the first group date wasn't awkward enough, we had to try on wedding dresses, and some of the women would be called to go up and take a photo with Matt at a round floral altar.

The first few women who went up were all over Matt. They didn't hesitate to kiss him, hug him, and emphatically pose. That was not my personality. So I just hoped I wouldn't be called up to pose. And I wasn't, but that didn't make the date any easier.

Matt would ask a question, and all the women around me would shout their responses. With my cochlear implant, all their voices blurred together, and I couldn't make out what anyone was saying, including Matt.

With my hearing loss, it was a tough environment for me to show my personality. I couldn't even answer Matt or process the group dates. There was no reason for Matt to fall for me if I couldn't show my personality around him. So I just had to hope that soon we'd get a quiet one-on-one date where we could get to know each other better.

But the hope of us getting that date died day after day, week after week. Not only did I not get the first one-on-one date, but I didn't get the second or the third. My time with Matt was brief on group dates. The more time that passed, the more stressed I became, thinking I wouldn't have my moment with him.

I continued to struggle a lot on the group dates due to my hearing loss. On one date, all the women read out poems they read for Matt, but I couldn't understand them over the chatter and laughter. Because of the lack of depth perception from sound with a cochlear implant, a girl laughing from across the room could make it hard for me to hear the woman on stage with a microphone. The voices competed with each other in my ear.

On another date, we had to row ourselves across a lake in large pumpkins. But at the time, I didn't have my Aqua Plus, a device that can go over a cochlear implant to make it waterproof. And I couldn't risk falling in the water with my cochlear implant, or I wouldn't be able to hear for the rest of the show. So, I had to take it off, which might not sound like a huge deal but it was daunting to navigate rowing a pumpkin boat in dead silence. I found myself constantly looking around to make sure nobody was coming up behind me. These difficulties on group dates meant that I was often more focused on getting through the dates than making a connection with Matt.

It didn't take long for the massive living quarters to feel small and suffocating. A lot of the things I was initially excited about, like the pool and the beautifully kept grounds, weren't even accessible. It was freezing outside, so there weren't a lot of outdoor activities. With no access to the internet or communication back home, boredom set in fast. I would do my nails often to pass the time, and then do the nails of the other women. I think I finished an entire booklet of Sudoku.

I think it would've been a difficult living situation no matter what, but it was especially hard for me with my cochlear implant. Just like when I stayed in the hotel prior to filming, I was almost never comfortable taking off my cochlear implant. Sure, I had Magi and there was always someone around to wake me, but I never wanted to rely on other people. To take off my implant was to give away some of my autonomy and place it in another person's hands. That wasn't something I was willing to do, being such an independent person.

But there were consequences to leaving my implant on all the time. The constant input of noise made me irritable because it wasn't what I was used to. I live for the brain breaks I get when I can finally take off my implant. The silence is peaceful, a way for me to center myself after a long day. And *The Bachelor* was a series of very long days, with not many breaks.

None of this was helped by the fact that I felt like I was

constantly being watched. Being on *The Bachelor* would've been tiring regardless, as the days were often really long, but feeling like I had to be on my best behavior at all times made the experience exhausting. At any point, something I said or did could be on national television.

But having Magi as a roommate definitely helped. At night, we would be completely alone, and we had some freedom to be honest about our feelings. We'd often offer each other advice about Matt, and weirdly, it didn't even feel like we were giving advice about the same guy most of the time. That's how different every woman's experience was on the show. My relationship with Matt was different from Magi's, and we had different approaches to dating him.

Magi liked Matt, but we both knew I was far more interested in him. Magi didn't love that she had to pursue Matt; it wasn't what she was used to culturally. But she became my big sister in the house. There was no animosity or jealousy about Matt. She'd calm me down if I was freaking out about not getting a date and reassure me of all I had to offer.

Magi, like me, had zero interest in getting involved with any house drama. If there was ever an uncomfortable moment with the girls or an argument was breaking out, Magi would ask me if I wanted to take a walk with her, and we'd both extricate ourselves from the situation.

That might have been why I was never aware of any of the drama that ended up on the show. I never heard any of the infighting, and nobody ever asked me about it. I was clueless to some of the things that were going on in the house between the other women.

My personal experience with the other girls was great though. I didn't have any real conflict with anyone. Aside from getting close to Magi, I spent a lot of time with Marylynn before she went home in the second week, and later, when Chelsea's roommate went home, I ended up spending a lot of time with her too.

Weeks passed, and at every rose ceremony, I received my rose yet didn't get asked on a date. At first, I just thought Matt and I had a strong connection, and he didn't need to explore it to know he was interested in me. But from talking to some of the other women, they also seemed to be building strong connections. So, what was going on?

I decided on my next group date, I was going to try to push the relationship forward. We'd had a lot of surface-level conversations, but I wanted more.

During our group date cocktail party, I sat down with Matt and began to tell him more personal details about my childhood.

"My birth dad did walk out on my mom, sister, and me right after we got our cochlear implants," I told him.

I think the audience's perception of this conversation was that my father left *because* of my hearing impairment, which couldn't be further from the truth. I just wanted to express to Matt that it's hard when a parent walks out, regardless of the reason, and it wasn't something I wanted my kids to have to face.

I took a deep breath before continuing. "When you have one of the most important people in your life walk out, it's hard not to wonder, if I open up to somebody, are they going to do the same?" It wasn't easy to say, and I hadn't been this vulnerable on a date in a long time. But I wanted to find out if this connection was real, and superficial conversation wasn't going to cut it.

"Can I tell you something?" Matt asked. "I can't imagine what that's like for you. But I can relate to not having a dad growing up and having a single mom who raised my older brother and me."

The ease between us allowed me to share something that I never had in a relationship before. Rarely while dating did I speak too deeply about my hearing loss. Discussing my disability always felt like walking a tightrope. It needed to be brought up, obviously, but it was a heavy subject. Normally, I'd never talk about my hearing loss too deeply after just a few dates, but I told Matt that there was a possibility that my children could be hard of hearing, and it was something I had to consider when planning a family. I wasn't sure if he was prepared for that. If I was going to evaluate a future with Matt, I had to know. And I wanted to see how he handled some of these more difficult discussions about my disability.

Matt explained that he had no regrets about being raised by a single mom, because it made him who he was. "And the barriers that you've had are things that I admire about you and encourage me to think about what a future with you would look like."

So many of my worries about our potential relationship were eased. We shared a kiss, and once again I was on cloud nine. It was just so easy to be around Matt. Sure, we hadn't gotten as much time together as I would've liked, but we had so much room to grow. Our superficial conversations held us back, and that conversation really pushed us forward.

And it seemed Matt felt the same. Because that night, he gave me the group date rose. I was so sure that our one-on-one date was just on the horizon. After all, it would be pretty crazy if I got the first impression rose and the first kiss without ever getting a date, right?

Well, that's the nature of *The Bachelor*. Things are unpredictable.

Chapter 13

As we approached the last couple weeks of *The Bachelor*, drama began to heat up in the house. I had missed all the drama so far thanks to the careful maneuvering from Magi, but it was hard not to hear Serena C. and Katie screaming at each other from the other room. I didn't involve myself and didn't much care who was right or wrong; I just desperately wanted some quiet.

Being at *The Bachelor* for weeks on end as a naturally introverted person was draining. I was aware of how I was constantly being watched, and the stress wasn't helped by the fact that I still hadn't had my one-on-one date with Matt.

I would often find Chelsea, and we'd lie down somewhere to chat. She became a big comfort to me on the show because when we'd unwind together, we'd often be left alone. Chelsea was my shield from the stress of feeling like at any moment I could be pulled away or pushed to get involved in any of the drama brewing.

It was also easier to focus on my connection to a few of the women, like Chelsea and Magi, than the group as a whole. Not just because I tend to be more introverted, but also because it was hard to talk to everyone in a group setting. I was often missing vital pieces of the conversation and covering up for it with a quick smile or laugh.

This actually got me in trouble on the show. At one point, the conversation with some of the women got a little nasty on camera, and the camera caught me laughing along. Some of the viewers picked up on this and thought I was playing the role of "mean girl." Though a small subset of deaf watchers recognized my laugh as one of discomfort, because it was something they themselves had done many times. It's easier to smile or chuckle to blend in than to ask people to repeat themselves, especially in a group setting where people are already talking over each other. I'd completely misheard what someone had said and was laughing as a polite cover-up.

Still, there were some benefits to missing group conversations. It also meant I got left out of group drama. Chelsea occasionally filled me in on the details but, really, I preferred not to know. Then I couldn't be implicated in any of it. I minded my business, enjoyed hanging out with Chelsea, and tried to focus on what I came here for.

I still had some hope Matt and I might connect, though the

excitement I had on night one had waned significantly. But this week, I was surely going to get a date. Katie, Jessenia, and I were the only ones to not have gone on a one-on-one date. And as the woman who got both the first impression rose and the first kiss, it only seemed natural he'd ask me out.

Katie got pulled for a one-on-one first. I was sure she'd come back home with a rose. But around midnight, there was a big commotion coming from downstairs. I crawled out of bed and went down to see what was going on.

A staff member was walking in to grab Katie's suitcases. For the very first time during our season, a contestant was sent home after a date.

The pressure was on.

Matt clearly had hometowns on his mind and was doing his best to curate a group of women he could actually see himself with. Would I make the cut? The women assured me that I'd get asked out on a date, and I was inclined to agree with them. Who gets the first impression rose and doesn't get a date?

There were two one-on-one dates the following week, and Jessenia and I were the only two not to have gone on one. I was sure we'd be getting those two dates. It was no surprise when the first one-on-one date card came for Jessenia.

But when the next card came, I waited with bated breath. It had to be my name. It just had to be.

"Serena P."

Hearing her name made my heart sink. But Serena had

already been on a date with Matt. How was she getting two dates, and I hadn't even gotten one? It was the moment I knew my journey at *The Bachelor* was over.

By this point, a lot of my feelings for Matt had lessened after weeks of minimal interaction, but I couldn't help feeling a little rejected. Why was I the only one to not get a one-on-one date?

I wasn't sure. All I knew was that I no longer wanted to be there. I was beyond ready to go home.

Some of the other women tried to comfort me.

"Maybe Matt doesn't need to have a date with you to know he wants to take you to hometowns," Chelsea suggested.

But that just didn't seem believable to me. We barely knew each other. We'd had no chance to determine compatibility.

My suspicions were confirmed when I went on my last group date. It became clear that Matt had front-runners. He seemed really into Michelle, Rachael, and Bri. It was no secret. He was fawning over them.

I decided to pull Matt aside to talk, though I wasn't exactly holding out hope that I'd get any clarity. I was pretty sure that even if I expressed my concerns, Matt was going to try to talk me into staying until the rose ceremony. That was the nature of the show. And I couldn't blame him for stringing me along, knowing that he was supposed to withhold a lot of his thoughts and feelings from the girls. It wouldn't make for good television if every woman he didn't have a connection with went home.

"I think from the very beginning, all I've really wanted is more time with you," I told him after we both took a seat. "It's scary because I can see the possibility of a future with you. Can you see the possibility of a future with me? I mean, I know you obviously can't say too much."

There was no smile on his face. "From night one, I was drawn to you. And I was so comfortable in our relationship that I explored other relationships. And in exploring those relationships with other women, I did grow strong feelings for them. If I'm being honest with you and following my heart, my heart is pulling me in another direction. I apologize."

I was surprised. Not because he turned me down—it was pretty obvious that rejection was coming—but because he was being so truthful. He could have strung me along for the show, got me to attend the next rose ceremony, but he didn't.

"I really do appreciate you being honest," I told him and meant it, as difficult as it was in the moment.

He walked me out, and the weight of everything hit me.

It wasn't like I was deeply in love with Matt. All we got were little blips together. But with all the pressure to connect, I'd been more honest with Matt about my life and my experiences with hearing loss than I ever had been while dating. And it stung that the honesty only led to rejection. I had always struggled so deeply with being vulnerable, especially in dating and particularly when it came to talking about my disability. This experience didn't exactly lead to me wanting to open up further.

But at least I didn't have to get rejected at the rose ceremony.

I could just go home. In the days prior, both Magi and Chelsea had been sent home, so I didn't have my close friends with me anymore. There was a lot of relief in leaving.

And even more relief in finally getting my phone back on the way to the airport. The first call I made was to my mom, something she made me promise I would do. When she picked up, I was in tears.

"I'm coming home, Mom."

"Oh, Abigail." Her voice was sympathetic. "We thought we might be coming for hometowns. They gave us a call to prepare."

I gave her the rundown as much as I could in our short call, and she did the same.

"I have to tell you, spoilers have come out that you got the first impression rose. There are already a lot articles out about you."

Well, that was coming, but I wasn't fully expecting to get attention until closer to the show's release. I was still processing everything, so I couldn't think about all the attention I'd gotten yet.

Though as soon as I hung up and started sorting through my social media, it became obvious I couldn't avoid that attention. People I hadn't spoken to since high school were messaging me. It was overwhelming to say the least. And outside of my close friends, I couldn't be sure which messages were genuine. Because people knew I had gotten the first impression rose, they believed there was a distinct possibility I got engaged on *The Bachelor*. I'd never been the kind of person to garner a lot of attention, so it was hard to believe that so many people actually wanted to reconnect with me.

But in the sea of new messages, I saw a familiar face. Chelsea had messaged me on Instagram.

"Hey girl. I don't know when you'll get this, but I wanted to make sure you had my number. Call me when you can."

After I got home, she was one of the few people I wanted to talk to. I basically slept at my parents' house for three days straight. The exhaustion built up from late nights on *The Bachelor* had gotten to me. But it was such a relief to go to sleep and know that when I woke up, I wasn't being recorded. When I had a knock at my door, I knew it was my mom, not somebody with an ulterior motive.

I missed my friends dearly, but I wasn't ready to talk to them right away. I knew that they'd want all the details and, for the most part, those details weren't going to make sense to them. I had always been so calm and collected when dating, cutting a guy off far before I got hurt. So how could I explain that I actually really liked Matt? That I was crying on the drive to the airport? They'd be so confused.

But they weren't in that environment. For the past month, every woman on *The Bachelor* ate, slept, and breathed Matt. It was the topic of every discussion. We'd get a date card every couple of days. It was so intense.

Now that I was home, I didn't feel those intense feelings at all. In fact, as soon as I got my phone back and was able to interact with the wider world, all my feelings dissipated quickly. It felt similar to when I went on a normal date with a guy that didn't work out. I was ready to move on to the next. But even that was hard to explain. How could I have cried over a guy that I now was no longer interested in at all?

Chelsea would understand though. I was so grateful she'd sent me her number, and I reached out to her pretty quickly. And she had discovered the same thing as me. For as extreme as emotions were running on the show, she was pretty relaxed now that she was home. I got so much peace from being able to lean on her now that this experience was over. While I was gone, I missed my girlfriends back home, but now that I was home, I was missing some of the intense bonds I'd made while filming.

After I'd gotten enough sleep and was ready to drop back into life, I started to read more of the information that had gotten out about me. At first, I thought it was kind of nice. So many people were reaching out, letting me know how my representation as a deaf contestant meant so much to them. It reaffirmed my decision to go on the show.

It didn't take long for the positive attention to turn sour though. I knew *The Bachelor* was popular, but I never fully grasped just how seriously people dig into contestants' lives on the show. Suddenly, people were looking up my voting record, finding my original birth certificate, and blasting my biological father's name online. As someone who was and is deeply private, this spurred a lot of anxiety in me.

Beyond anxiety, I was dealing with some guilt. Because they weren't just digging up my past; they were digging up my mom's past too. My family was supportive of me, but they didn't sign up to be on the show and certainly didn't sign up to have their lives thoroughly examined. The divorce was something my mom had dealt with decades ago. She never complained, but I still felt awful that it was being brought up.

There was nothing I could do though. I had agreed to go on the show, for better or worse. And it was going to get worse when the show came out.

I put my energy into focusing on what I wanted to do with my life now. Before going on the show, I let my previous employer know I'd be gone in case they tried to get a hold of me. They wished me luck and told me to get in touch when I was home. I did, and thankfully, they were bringing some employees back on. I was invited to work remotely for them.

The remote work was a blessing because my lease with Rachel was almost up, and I didn't want to stay in Portland. Neither did my friend Jennah, who was interested in a move to New York. Chelsea was already living in New York, and I loved the idea of being closer to her. I agreed to relocate with Jennah, and we scheduled the move the same week *The Bachelor* premiered.

Probably not the best planning on my part. The first and second episodes were when I got the most airtime, so there were a lot of different requests for interviews and whatnot. It wasn't easy getting back to people while moving across the country.

Before I left for New York, I had a premiere party with my family and some of my closest friends at an Airbnb with a large living room where we could all gather around the TV with a few drinks. We were watching on West Coast time, and people on the other side of the country had already watched the episode. I promised myself I wouldn't be on my phone during the launch party, but once the comments started rolling in, it became impossible not to check them out.

And, man, there were *so many* of them. I watched my follower count go up in a way I never even imagined. I had seventy thousand new followers by the end of that first night and more notifications than I could ever read.

I'd been nervous about this night for a while, but it wasn't until the episode aired that the gravity of it all hit me. What had I done? What had I gotten myself into?

It goes without saying that I was already pretty amped up before *The Bachelor* came on. On top of the shocking amount of social media attention I was receiving, there was an awkwardness in watching the show with all my girlfriends and parents. Not a lot of people experience a room full of their closest friends and family watching them kiss a near stranger on television. So take my word for it, it's awkward. But everyone was incredibly supportive, especially my parents, despite them being pretty conservative about public displays of affection. They were so supportive, in fact, that when I visited them the following day, they asked if I wanted to watch the episode again.

"You guys want to watch the whole thing again?" I asked. "But we just watched it last night."

"Well, yeah, but your friends were all so excited and cheering for you that it was hard to hear. We would love to see it again," Mom said.

I laughed and agreed to watch it with them. It was a lot less nerve-racking the second time around since I knew what to expect.

The first few days before my move, I spent a lot of time going through my social media while trying to process the fact that I was now in the limelight. Before the show, I didn't even have a thousand followers. I posted a photo maybe once a month or so, and it was just for my friends.

I had no intention of being an influencer after *The Bachelor*, so this world was all new to me. I know everyone always says that, and when looking at my life now, that statement may be laughable. But it was true. I went on *The Bachelor* for the experience. I had no faith that I could keep up the influencer lifestyle aesthetic. Though these days, people don't necessarily have to keep up that lifestyle to maintain a following. But this was when TikTok was just starting to take off, which allowed for a new type of influencer, where people could focus on any niche and find a potential audience. I was still stuck on the idea of the typical Instagram influencer. You know, the ones who were posting travel photos, meal shots, and their perfectly curated wardrobe. That wasn't me.

The biggest adjustment was having to deal with the negative comments. While some people commended my presence on *The*

Bachelor as a deaf woman, many others were frustrated that I was the face of deaf representation. A lot of people said they would've preferred to see someone from the capital-*D* deaf community. And I can't blame them for that. It's only natural to want more representation.

But I felt personally attacked. I never once tried to claim that I was representing the deaf community at large. Obviously, I wasn't in charge of casting. I was the one on screen though. So the negativity was thrown onto me.

I had to develop thick skin fast. It was an adjustment. But I held my head high and hoped that as the season progressed, people would see I wasn't trying to be representative of the Deaf community. And sure enough, as the show progressed, those comments faded. Still, navigating social media was a brand-new hurdle that I didn't think much about when I was on the show.

So when my now manager, Lori, reached out to me, I was in desperate need of some guidance. Though admittedly, I didn't quite understand why she wanted to represent me.

"I'm sorry, but I just don't see how you'd be able to make money off of me. I'm hardly an influencer."

"Let me help you figure that out," she assured me.

She wasn't kidding when she said she'd help me. Even though I couldn't pay her anything for a while, she assisted me in curating my social media presence. I had all these followers and no idea how to interact with them, but Lori had so many tips. With her guidance, I tried to wrap my head around making income using social media. But it still took a little convincing at first. I had my taste of the limelight, but I was pretty sure I didn't want to stay in it.

And I knew I didn't want to do any more *Bachelor* shows. As grateful as I was for the opportunity, the show had been grueling. When the producers called to offer me a spot on *Bachelor in Paradise*, I declined straight away.

I didn't decline the offer just because of how difficult filming had been the first time around. I also had a lot of insecurities that the only reason they kept me on *The Bachelor* so long was to use me as a token of deaf representation. That wasn't what I wanted to do. I was already the deaf *Bachelor* contestant, I wasn't going to be the deaf *Bachelor in Paradise* contestant too.

After moving to New York, I started spending a lot more time with Chelsea. Shortly after my arrival, Chelsea and I were invited to a *Bachelor* party with some of the guys from Tayshia and Clare's seasons. Chelsea was pretty sure she wanted to go on *Bachelor in Paradise*, and the party was a way to mingle with other contestants. Even though I didn't want to do *Paradise*, I was supportive of her and tagged along.

But I regretted it pretty soon after our arrival. Chelsea was mingling with some of the guys, which was no surprise; she was a hot commodity. But that left me alone for the most part. Since I wasn't doing *Paradise*, the guys didn't really have any interest in me. And though plenty of them were nice people, I wasn't interested in them either. I was only there to play wingwoman for Chelsea, and I could only do that for so long until I started to get bored.

I texted Jennah asking her to come keep me company, then gave her the address to the party. She agreed, but she'd be a while, so I had to entertain myself for a bit.

Chelsea and some of the others wanted to move to the rooftop, so I followed them. But I was in pretty high heels, and the stairs up to the rooftop were a grated metal material. You can probably see where this is heading.

My heels got caught in the holes of the grate and my entire body flung forward. It wasn't a gentle fall either. I scraped my elbows and my knees and broke a nail.

Now I really wasn't having fun. Ivan and Jordan were kind enough to help me up, get me past the stairs, and give me a Corona beer to ice my knee. But I was still pretty embarrassed and ended up sitting on my own in one of the rattan chairs.

I searched the rooftop for a place I'd be more comfortable, and my eyes landed on Noah in a hammock by himself. The hammock seemed nice actually. Maybe it would take some pressure off my knee. I headed that way.

"Hey, is this spot taken?" I ask.

"No, go right ahead."

I sat down next to him. "Hey, aren't you a nurse?"

"Yeah, why?" He stared at me.

"Then why didn't you try to help me with my traumatic fall on the stairs? I could've died!" I teased him.

"You fell? I didn't even notice."

Well, that made me feel a little better. I thought the whole party had witnessed my clumsiness.

We chatted for a bit, and he was sweet. But to be quite honest, I friendzoned him pretty quickly. He was nice, but he didn't take a ton of initiative in the conversation. I'd always been attracted to men who were willing to go after what they wanted.

Alright, let's just call it what it is. I was attracted to douchebags. I had a thing for bad boys, which was probably why I hadn't had a lasting relationship since high school. Noah didn't strike me as a bad guy.

Though after we met, I went back and watched Tayshia's season and was surprised to find Noah was portrayed as a villain in the show. Super unhealthy, I know, but this may have piqued my interest in him a little more.

I didn't want to continue dating douchebags though. The months after *The Bachelor* were a period of rapid growth and self-reflection for me. I was finally ready to actually settle into a relationship, and I wasn't going to get into that relationship by going after bad boys. It was a huge reason I didn't want to do *Paradise*. It was such an intense way to date, one that often led to a lot of drama. Never again did I want to cry on television. And it's hard to form a healthy, happy relationship amidst reality TV drama. So if I wasn't sure a serious relationship could form on *Paradise*, and I didn't want to be the token deaf girl, it didn't seem like I had a place there.

Noah messaged me a few weeks after we met.

"You going to *Paradise*?" he asked.

"Definitely not. Are you?"

"Yes. Why aren't you going?"

I saw no reason not to be honest. "I don't want to deal with the drama of it all. I'm content where I'm at." And I was. I still wasn't sure I wanted to do the influencer thing. I liked my job. I loved New York. Why bother shaking things up?

"Well, if I have a margarita and a hammock waiting for you, would you come?"

I've always been a sucker for flirty banter. "Sure. Get a hammock and I'll be there."

Only a few short days later, the producers called again. This time, with the promise that some of the guys really wanted to meet me.

I was pretty sure *some of the guys* meant only Noah. But I wasn't opposed to meeting him too.

"Abigail, seriously. What do we have to do to get you down here?" one of the producers asked.

With Noah's interest, the producers' willingness to negotiate, and Chelsea begging me to go, I broke down. I mean, it was just a few weeks. It was like a vacation. I'd leave for a few weeks, then come back to my regularly scheduled life. What could possibly happen in just a few weeks?

More than I could ever have imagined, as it turned out.

Chapter 14

I had no idea I was going to be the first one to walk onto the beach on *Paradise*. Being on *The Bachelor* hadn't made me any more comfortable being on national television. I had a bit of anxiety brewing when I walked down the steps, but that anxiety exploded when I saw who was waiting to interview me.

David Spade was waiting for me halfway down the steps to the beach in a blue button-down shirt. I was warned that we'd have celebrity hosts this season, but I figured that meant people from other seasons of *The Bachelor*.

My dad was a superfan of David Spade. We'd watched all his movies together. Needless to say, I was starstruck. Besides Chris Harrison, I still hadn't met any other celebrities. And this wasn't just any celebrity. David Spade was a staple in our household. My dad was going to lose his mind!

"Oh my god, I'm actually shaking right now," I told him with a laugh.

David was great at keeping the mood light though. Within a minute, I was feeling a little calmer. Talking to him felt more natural than I thought. Until he told me I was going to be the first one to the beach.

"No, no!" I covered my face with my hands quickly.

"Why is that a bad thing?" he asked.

"I like to walk and talk to people right away because I'm always so nervous!" It was a little anxiety inducing knowing that the cameras would all be focused on me. There was no possibility for me to blend into the crowd like I'd usually try to do.

But at least for a moment I got to be the only person taking in the gorgeous view of the beach. It really did look like paradise.

Joe was the next person to come down, and honestly, I didn't think he was a contestant. I knew him from previous seasons of the show and assumed he was here to help host or do something else on the show. When he told me he was here to find love like everyone else, I was surprised. He told me he was interested in meeting Serena Pitt.

It didn't take long for them to send down Ivan, who also had his eye on Serena. *Here it goes. Let the drama begin.* Already, I wasn't sure whether or not I was ready for what the next few weeks would bring.

There was both relief and a little anxiety when Serena walked down. Finally, someone I knew and was comfortable with. But how were things going to go down with multiple men vying for her attention?

I did my best to mingle, and I really did have an open mind coming on *Paradise*. But I didn't seem to have much of a connection with any of the men on the beach, and they didn't seem like they had much of a connection with me either. I was starting to get in my head, worrying that the men were chalking me up as "the deaf girl."

Then came Noah.

Obviously, because of our previous chats, as brief as they were, he had piqued my interest. I still wasn't sure if he'd be assertive enough for me though.

The bad boys weren't for me, I knew that. I wanted to take a different approach to dating. Bad boys don't make great husbands. Still, I needed a guy who would chase after me a little.

Despite how reserved he was the first time we met, Noah took me by surprise. He asked me to talk right away. There was no hesitation. He knew what he wanted and went for it.

The assertiveness definitely was a turning point in my feelings toward him. Despite what I saw on Tayshia's season, Noah was no villain. It was obvious to me from the very first conversation that he was a sweetheart. Funny, attractive, willing to show me that he wanted me. He was checking off all the boxes.

And there was a natural comfort between us from the very start. We were able to joke with each other like we'd been friends for years, even though we'd only had like two conversations prior to *Paradise*.

Though I knew there'd still be more men coming and was

open to other sparks, on that first night, there was nobody but Noah who caught my interest. So when I got my date card, it was a no-brainer who I'd pick.

The date played out awkwardly on television, but I can assure you, it was far more awkward in real life. By the time we were going out on our date, it had already been a very long day. If we weren't on *Paradise*, I would've been asleep already. The excitement of the date helped to keep me awake, but I was nearing zombie mode.

On top of being tired, this was my very first one-on-one date on television. The lack of experience made me nervous. But Noah really stepped up for me. He could see I was out of my element and guided me on the date in both activities and conversation. It was the first sign that this might be a guy who could anticipate my needs and be there for me.

But it was still just a first date, and I didn't want to get too heavy. Truth be told, the conversations with each other were so easy, that I was already falling pretty hard. I didn't want to scare him off or have a similar situation to my time on *The Bachelor*. I didn't want to have an amazing first night that fizzled out into nothing and only led to disappointment.

I was guarded. Just like I was when I'd dated back home. The nice thing about *Paradise* is it much more resembled normal dating than *The Bachelor*. And because it was so much more like regular dating, my normal dating habits made an appearance. I didn't want to open up too much because I wasn't ready to get hurt.

And the chances of getting hurt on *Paradise* were sky-high. At any point, a new person could come in and swoop up the guy we'd been dating. I might have to see Noah go on dates and kiss other women. It was hard to fully open up to him not knowing what difficulties were waiting for us just around the corner.

I was hopeful though. The awkwardness of the date didn't make me doubt my affections for Noah at all. If anything, his comfort during such an awkward situation had me even more interested.

The next day we got to talking again, but since the men had the roses, more women were showing up on the beach. Noah had been very honest with me about the fact that he was going all in on this process. As interested as he was in me, he wanted to really give his all to *Paradise* to see if he could find his person. And I wanted to do the same.

But when Demi came down, I realized how difficult it was going to be to watch Noah go on a date.

Demi was really cute, high-energy, and funny. As soon as she arrived, I was worried she would pull Noah for her date, because he could match her humor. If she did, I had no doubt he'd say yes and fully explore his options. What might a date between them bring? I didn't want to think about it.

I was practically holding my breath when Demi came out to announce who she wanted to take out.

"Brendan, would you like to go on this date with me?"

Phew. I was in the clear. I could get used to having Noah to myself.

And to my surprise, I did. More women would come down onto the beach, but they'd never ask for Noah. He gave me his rose, and the next week when more men came down, nobody asked me on a date. In that way, Noah and I had it kind of easy.

Nothing is truly easy in paradise though. Every day Noah and I got closer, often spending our time talking and cuddled up on one of the daybeds. Just like on *The Bachelor*, it was easier for me to choose to spend time with Noah and a couple girlfriends I'd made on the show because the group setting made it so hard to hear. This meant that we got close very fast. We'd talk about our lives and what we wanted out of the show. Joking was effortless with us. Hanging out with Noah was just easy.

As much as my time on *The Bachelor* had been about my hearing loss, I didn't feel that way on *Bachelor in Paradise*, and that was primarily thanks to Noah. He already knew I had a cochlear implant, so he didn't ask about it. But he also didn't dance around the subject either. He let me know I could tell him about it whenever I wanted, but he also didn't have any questions in particular. And he'd anticipate my needs before I even had to voice them. He would repeat to me what the host was saying before the rose ceremony.

"Is it a little hard for you to hear right now?" he'd ask when we sat in large groups.

"Kind of," I'd sometimes admit.

"Come on, we can go sit over there."

Noah did exactly what I'd always wanted a partner to. He saw me for me but didn't pretend my disability didn't exist. And because he saw me so completely, I knew the audience would too. My fears about being the deaf contestant were assuaged. With Noah, some of my personality was brought out. I hoped that with this season, people would see me more completely.

Noah was almost too good to be true. So naturally, I had to do a bit of self-sabotaging.

I've always been bad about comparing myself to others, and *Bachelor in Paradise* really brings out the worst of this trait. Every day, we were surrounded by other couples. I had to watch them get hot and heavy with each other. People would talk about how passionately they felt about their dating partner, and I'd wonder why Noah and I weren't progressing at that same pace.

We had such a deep comfort with each other, but that intense lust wasn't present. Some of the couples couldn't keep their hands off each other, and that wasn't Noah and me.

We had a conversation early on, making it clear that neither of us were going to go to the boom boom room. There were cameras in there, and that wasn't a part of our relationship we needed to explore on television. So there was an understanding that we'd move slower. Shouldn't we still be so attracted to each other that we wanted to engage in some hot and heavy make-out sessions? We had just met, so if we weren't expressing our affection physically so early on in our relationship, did it mean we didn't have what it took to leave *Paradise* as a couple? It felt almost like we were friendzoning each other.

In retrospect, my concerns seem so silly. It's just the nature of being forced into close proximity with so many other couples. Of course, I'd be comparing myself when I had to watch other couples making out all day long.

Noah was lying down on one of the lounge chairs, and I sat next to him, a drink in hand.

He looked up. "What's up?"

"I don't know." I probably should've thought about the best way to word this but the words just kind of spilled out. "I'm wondering what you want out of our situationship?"

He seemed caught off guard straightaway. "Well, obviously I like you. We're solid. We're fun. Everyone is obsessed with our relationship."

"Well, that's what I'm struggling with. I feel like we make a lot of sense. And to everyone else, we make a lot of sense. So why are we holding back?"

Silence from Noah. Little did I know, he was already misinterpreting what I was getting at.

"I love that it's so easy between us, but it's kind of a blessing and a curse, you know?" I tried to explain further.

"Do you think we're like, just friends at the end of this?" Noah asked.

"I think we're more than friends; we're just not at a relationship level yet."

"I don't normally kiss my friends," Noah said with a twinge of sarcasm. "But at the end of the day, we need to be more than friends."

"I just feel like maybe you stopped trying." It was true that I didn't feel pursued as much as the first few days we shared on the beach.

"It's not that I stopped trying. But a minute ago is the first time I've even heard you say that you liked me. I feel like I do things and don't get much of a response."

Watching the show back, it became so obvious what he was talking about. It wasn't obvious at the time though. The conversation did not end well, with Noah believing that I wanted to end the relationship.

I panicked. Had I just screwed up a really good thing?

Communication wasn't our strong suit during *Paradise*, and it was something we had to work on even after we left the show. During that first conflict, neither of us seemed to get where the other was coming from, and we certainly didn't end up with the same conclusion. Noah took a long walk on the beach, mulling over the end of our relationship.

Thankfully, Noah didn't walk away. We were able to have another conversation where I admitted I wasn't communicating well. What I wanted to express in my head and what came out of my mouth were two very different stories. And Noah let me know his concerns that I was very guarded, and I was.

"I'll definitely work on communicating better," I told him.

"So far, I've loved getting to know you. There's potential there, and moving forward, I want to continue to pursue this. What are your thoughts?"

"My thoughts? Honestly, I thought I screwed this up. And it really made me realize how much I care about you."

I loved the soft smile that formed on his face. "You still wanna be the power couple of the beach?" he asked.

"Royalty," I jokingly corrected him.

"Royalty," he agreed.

We'd gotten past our first-ever fight, and my feelings for Noah were stronger than ever. If we could get through this, I could really see us leaving the beach together. It was clear we were both in this. What other hurdles could *Paradise* throw at us, with one week left on the beach?

I never could've predicted that I'd leave *Paradise* in tears, swearing that I never wanted to speak to Noah again.

Chapter 15

N oah and I made an agreement fairly early on that we weren't going to say, "I love you," on *Paradise*. We also didn't want to get engaged. As much as we wanted to continue our relationship after *Paradise*, we wanted to do things in a more conventional way. We needed to meet each other's families, spend some time in the real world, before we took those big steps.

So you can imagine my surprise when I heard Noah say he was falling in love with me.

We were lying on a daybed, having a serious discussion about the future of our relationship after *Paradise*.

"I just want to be completely transparent. That's really the only way to do it, put it all out there," Noah said with his arm wrapped around me. "I think the only reason it's hard for me is because I more than like you. I'm falling in love with you, and I can see it working in the real world."

The words came out of his mouth so casually that I thought it was an accident. He froze up a little after, and in my head, he had just accidentally told me he loved me. It didn't seem to be on purpose, especially after our discussions about how we wouldn't say the L word on camera.

Immediately, my mind was going a mile a minute. I definitely was falling in love with him too, and in any other situation, I would've told him so right away.

Except I was pretty sure he had just said something he didn't want to say out loud on television. And the last thing I wanted to do was put him on the spot. So I moved past it, like I assumed he wanted me to. We'd have plenty of chances to say this to each other after *Paradise*, or so I thought.

I walked away from the conversation feeling pretty good. *Paradise* was soon coming to a close. Noah and I were in an amazing place, and now I knew he was falling as hard for me as I was for him. I was sure we were going to leave the beach together.

I could never have predicted what would happen next.

Serena and I saw the sign for prom night first. When it was announced that we'd be doing an eighties-themed prom night, I was kind of excited. A themed prom night seemed fun. I was down to get dressed up in a corny 'eighties prom dress.

But prom night was my first clue that there was trouble in *Paradise*. The guys were all coming up with promposals, and I fully expected Noah to ask me. When he didn't, my mind went back to our last conversation. Had he meant to say what he said? I wasn't sure.

Until Serena confirmed it for me. "So, Noah told me that he said he loved you, and you didn't respond?" Serena asked as we were getting dressed up.

"He said that?"

"Yeah, he seemed pretty worried."

Oh, no. So he had meant to say it. As soon as I realized my mistake, all I wanted to do was go and tell Noah I was falling for him too.

But there was almost no time for us to talk. Everyone was getting ready for prom, and once we arrived, there was way too much going on. I decided I was absolutely going to tell Noah I was falling for him too. No longer did I care about the cameras being around. I just wanted him to know how I felt.

Still, I didn't have much doubt that we'd be leaving the beach together. This was just a small rift, and I'd fix it when we got a chance to talk. We were still a solid couple.

And apparently everyone else on the beach thought so too, because during prom superlatives, we got voted most likely to live happily ever after. But after our award was announced, I felt some tension from Noah.

When he asked if we could speak privately, I figured that would be my chance to clear everything up.

We took a seat on the stairs. Noah looked down at the ground before he started speaking.

"I don't know if you could tell, but there's been a conflict between what I feel and what I think I should do. I've built strong feelings for you, and it's taken me off guard, to be honest. But I feel like I've been trying to force something that I want when deep down I don't know if you're my person."

My heart sank.

"I don't think I've ever been this blindsided before. How do you go from telling someone you're in love with them the night before to this conversation?" I asked.

"What I said last night is still true. But I don't want to force something."

"Well, I feel like you're a little late in being honest." I was shutting down. No part of me wanted to be having this conversation.

In the course of talking, it hit me that this was going to be on national television. Once again, the entire world would see my rejection. But this time would be so much worse.

With Matt, I knew we weren't connecting. We never really built up a relationship. But it was so different with Noah. I thought we were one of the strongest couples on the beach. Everyone did. We were planning to date after *Paradise*. This came out of nowhere.

"I've lost sleep over this," Noah said.

"I mean, I really don't know what you want me to say. I'm confused. It seemed like you were pushing me to get to your level, but obviously you've had this feeling for more than twenty-four hours, yet you still chose to say you were falling in love with me."

"This has nothing to do with you."

"I know it has nothing to do with me. I didn't do anything to be blamed for." When I said this, I believed it wholeheartedly.

In the moment, I was so angry with Noah. I felt played by him. It was easy for me to feel betrayed when, from my point of view, his doubt came out of nowhere.

It wasn't until later, when I was able to watch the show back, that things started to click. While we were filming, I didn't see myself as being withholding, but after the fact it became clear that I did play a part in our relationship deteriorating. I hadn't been as open with him as he was with me, and that created a barrier. At the end of the day, it was a big miscommunication that led to this awful moment.

But it was so hard to see that while I was experiencing it.

I wanted nothing more than to run away from *Paradise* in that moment. I knew then and there that I was done with the show. If it was over between me and Noah, I wanted to go home.

Leaving *Bachelor* was so much more difficult the second time around. Even in our brief time together, I became closer with Noah than I had with any other man I dated. I was head over heels for the guy. I believed he was the real deal. Having to leave *Paradise* without him was heartbreaking, more so because I didn't see it coming.

Normally, I wouldn't have been allowed to have my phone right away, but I insisted on calling my mom.

As soon as I heard her pick up, I broke down in tears. I told her everything. Although, she already knew Noah and I were dating because of a spoiler that had been released.

"I just can't believe he ambushed me on TV," I told her. "I am never speaking to him again." And when I said it, I meant it.

I expected Mom to agree with me, to be as angry as I was, but her words surprised me. "Abigail, I wouldn't write him off completely yet. He seems like a sweet guy, and you're in a really weird environment."

It isn't what I expected to hear, but it did soften me a bit. Mom knows me better than anyone and wants the best for me. So the fact that she didn't immediately take my side was my first clue that I wasn't seeing the full picture.

And she was right. Reality television is such a weird situation. Most of our communication issues stemmed from the fact that we were being filmed. We were trying to be so careful about what we said. It wasn't a normal dating environment.

"Just see how the next few weeks play out," Mom advised.

"Okay. But I'm not texting or calling him." I was still insistent that I was the wronged party, and if anyone was going to reach out, it had to be him to me.

It didn't take long for Noah to contact me. I was on a layover on my way home when I got his text, though it wasn't what I was hoping for.

"I'm really sorry for the way that happened. I never wanted to hurt you, and I definitely didn't want to do it on TV."

It was apologetic but pretty neutral. He was apologizing for hurting me, but it wasn't like he wanted to give us a chance or anything, and I still did.

"What happened? I thought you were going to be open and honest with me," I texted back.

"Can I call you to talk more when you get home? There's a lot I didn't want to say on television."

I agreed. Though I knew I'd be exhausted when I got back, I wanted to hear him out. I still didn't think he'd be able to convince me he wasn't being malicious, but on our call he surprised me.

"I felt like I was trying to get you to open up to me all season. When you didn't, I had my doubts that you were really my person," he explained.

And that made sense. I knew I could be aloof when dating. I definitely didn't mean to brush him off when he said he was falling in love with me, but I think that was the last straw for Noah. Me withholding my feelings built up slowly through our time on *Paradise*.

"Well, I was planning to tell you I was falling in love with you at prom. I just didn't get the chance," I told him.

We laid it all out. By the end of the call, I did understand his perspective, and I no longer considered him a villain in this situation. Still, neither of us talked about dating. The relationship stayed off.

We continued to text and call throughout the next week, but as friends. At first, I enjoyed this, because I really missed him when I got home. But eventually, it became too much to bear.

"I don't think I can keep talking like this," I told Noah over the phone. "We're chatting like nothing happened, but I'm still reeling from the breakup. I need some space."

Noah was really understanding of this, agreeing to step back and let me heal from the emotional roller coaster that just happened.

But just three days later, he was calling again. This time with a proposition.

"Look, I really miss you, Abigail. Is there any way we could meet in person and see if there's still potential here?"

I felt the same exact way. When I told my family that Noah wanted to meet up, I was surprised that my parents suggested we use the family cabin. My parents are usually very traditional and wouldn't like me staying over with a boyfriend. But they seemed to really like Noah and wanted us to give it a shot.

Noah flew out to Oregon, and that's when we really found paradise. Without cameras around, we were able to talk to each other without filters. And as good as we'd been on the beach, we were even better when we weren't being filmed.

Our relationship came naturally to us. We were incredibly comfortable with each other. By the end of that trip, I knew that this was something great. Before he went home, Noah asked if I'd be his girlfriend, and I agreed.

We had to be sneaky though. We weren't allowed to talk or post about our relationship until *Bachelor in Paradise* premiered. Which meant we couldn't really go out in public. I visited him a lot in Tulsa, since coming to my place was out of the question. New York was far too busy, and we couldn't risk being spotted.

We'd also spend a lot of time in Tulsa with his family and friends. We'd do days at the lake, bonfires, and so many movie nights. Movie nights were easy because there was no way we could be spotted. We had to get creative about how we could keep our privacy, and Noah ended up getting his car windows tinted so I could drive around town with him but stay in the car if he had to go inside a store or something.

One evening, we decided to grab some sushi, and Noah parked in front of the restaurant. I stayed behind per usual, but as soon as the driver's side door shut, a few girls walked out of the sushi place.

"Wait, oh my god," a petite brunette girl nearly shouted, "You're Noah! From *Bachelor in Paradise*!"

"That's me," Noah smiled.

"We loved you on the show!" One of the other girls was grinning at him. "Are you still with Abigail?"

Noah only shrugged. "I don't know. Guess you're going to have to finish the show to find out."

Little did they know, I was right there, watching the whole conversation unfold.

I look back so fondly at this time in our relationship. It was amazing to spend so much time in Tulsa hanging out with his family. Most of our days were spent on his brother's ranch, riding ATVs, watching the sunset together. It was simple, and I realized that through all the chaos of *The Bachelor*, this was what I wanted. This was where I was happiest, doing simple activities with Noah.

It was just him and me, living in our own little world. The show wasn't out yet, so we didn't have to worry about the world reacting to our relationship. We had time to build a foundation without the input of anyone else. And we built a really strong one, which came in handy once the show actually did come out.

Reliving our relationship was not easy, especially when everyone had their own opinions on it. I got a lot more criticism on *Paradise* than I did during Matt's season, making me feel psychoanalyzed with every little move I made. And a lot of the comments were really harsh.

Noah was a rock for me during this time. He stood by me, and even rewatching our mistakes played back to us did not create doubt in either of us. Once we were off the beach, there was no more doubt in our relationship.

Needless to say, I struggled with this. I tried to avoid comments as much as possible, but it's easier said than done. Noah could see I was getting stuck in my head.

"Hey, I'm taking you somewhere," he told me one evening.

He dropped everything to grab a bottle of wine and take me for a long drive. We unplugged for the entire day, no phones, just us. We parked in the middle of nowhere and popped the bottle of wine.

"The show will finish airing soon, and everything will be old news," Noah assured me. "And once it is, we can start our real lives together."

We spent the day just talking about our plans for the future. And it was so easy to picture that future.

All my life, I've been fiercely independent. Not wanting to ask for accommodations, not wanting to be seen as the deaf girl who needed help. But by being so independent and pushing away my deafness, I wasn't fully myself. Noah changed that.

My relationship with Noah was the first time I was really, truly myself. It took a while for me to let my guard down, obviously. Me not fully opening up was a huge source of conflict on *Paradise*. I knew I really liked Noah though, and if I was going to give this relationship a chance, I had to approach it differently. I couldn't be the same cool, aloof Abigail that I'd been in past relationships.

I allowed Noah to see the parts of me I never let any other man see. And it was effortless because of his nurturing nature. Noah became more than my partner; he was my advocate. He'd make sure I never forgot my cochlear implant accessories when we'd travel. If we were going to somewhere with a pool or beach, he'd make sure I had my Aqua Plus, a cover for my cochlear implant that makes it waterproof. When we're in a group setting and he notices I'm not hearing everyone, he makes sure I stay in the loop.

With him, I don't have to be so independent. I can just be me and know that I have him on my side. And when the dust settled after *Paradise* stopped airing, the relationship was as effortless as I hoped it would be.

So when my lease was up, we decided to move in together. Living together was not something we took lightly. The both of us agreed we would only move in with a partner if it was very serious. But we were serious about each other. And neither of us could handle long distance any longer.

Noah had a nursing contract in California, so we decided to find a place together there. I was a little nervous to tell my traditional parents about this, but once again, they surprised me. My parents loved Noah, and they wanted us to do whatever it took to make our relationship work. Everyone knew the distance was hard for us and was happy we'd get this opportunity to grow closer.

With Noah, I feel completely seen. Noah doesn't disregard my disability, and it isn't all he sees when looks at me.

I knew pretty quickly after moving in together that Noah was the one I wanted to spend my life with, but we both wanted to take it slow, despite the whole world dying to know when we'd finally get married. It was probably the most-asked question I got on Instagram. It's funny. We'd only been together a few months after *Paradise*—a time frame most people would consider pretty short for an engagement—but since we were on *The Bachelor*, everyone expected marriage fast. After all, many people on the show walk away engaged in a matter of weeks. But we knew that just wasn't for us.

Noah and I wanted to take things slower, explore, have some adventures, and we did. Noah has been working as a travel nurse, allowing us to live in different places and take time to travel in between his contracts. Most recently, we lived in beautiful San Diego with my sister. It was in San Diego that I realized, as much fun as we'd had moving around, I was ready to settle down somewhere, plant some roots. Noah was feeling the same way, so we decided we'd move to Oklahoma. Noah has family out there, and it's a really affordable place to buy a home. That was what I wanted, a home to call my own and decorate exactly as I wanted.

I found the perfect place, made an offer, and it became mine. It's a bit of a fixer-upper, but that's part of the fun. Noah and I couldn't wait to gut it and renovate it together.

When I closed on the house, we had a few weeks left in San Diego, but I got the itch to go. I asked Noah how he felt about leaving early and getting started on renovations, which he agreed to. I was a little surprised because, honestly, I thought he might be planning to propose in San Diego.

We'd talked about marriage extensively—as I think all couples should before they take that leap—and we were both ready. Noah wanted to make sure I got the ring of my dreams, so we picked out a design together, meaning I was well aware that he already had my engagement ring. I know some people prefer to be surprised, but if I was going to wear that ring for the rest of my life, I wanted to make sure I loved it! Besides, the engagement moment would still be a surprise. He bought the ring in February, but by summer, he still hadn't popped the question.

I was sure he'd do it in San Diego; it's such a beautiful location. But since I was springing a last-minute move on him, I knew there'd be no time to make plans for a proposal. And if he already had proposal plans, he wouldn't have agreed to move early. But I didn't mind either way. In a few weeks, my family was going to visit to see the new house. I figured Noah wanted to have my family around, and I was in no rush. The new house was plenty commitment enough for me.

The week we planned to leave, Noah was sitting on the couch with me and looked up from his phone. "Hey, Becca and Thomas want to do a farewell dinner this weekend."

"That sounds great," I agreed. "Where at?"

"At their friend's condo on the beach. They wanna cook for us."

"Perfect."

We'd spent a lot of time with Becca and Thomas in San Diego since they were nearby, and I was definitely going to miss them. Thomas and Noah had grown especially close, so it was no surprise when they wanted to work out together before dinner. I hung back and got ready for one last beachside dinner before we moved to Tulsa.

Since I'd just bought a house, I was enamored with the beachside condo once we arrived. I couldn't help myself, opening cabinets and closets, being just a tad bit nosy. But it was a beautiful condo! And the ocean view really sealed the deal. It was a perfect place for a farewell dinner.

"Maybe you shouldn't be opening all the doors like that," Noah suggested, a little tense. Which I didn't fully understand, but I shrugged it off.

"Come on, let's go on the patio," Noah suggested.

That was fine by me. I did want to see the beach.

Things got weirder when we stepped outside. Without warning, Noah grabbed my drink and bag and set them down. And he offered absolutely no explanation. Did this beach have some weird no-drink policy I wasn't aware of?

But when we stepped forward, I finally understood. Loads of rose petals sat atop a blue- and white-striped rug. The smile on my face was absolutely uncontainable. The ocean peeked out from the glass on the patio, serving as a beautiful backdrop for the moment where we'd make a lifelong commitment to each other.

The tears were filling my eyes before Noah even spoke.

"Abigail Heringer, will you marry me?"

"Yes," I had to choke out the word through tears.

"You sure?" Noah teased. Because it wouldn't be Noah if he didn't get at least one joke in there.

But I was sure. More sure than I'd ever been of any decision in my life.

After I said yes, friends came out to greet and congratulate us. The reason Noah was so nervous about me exploring the condo was because he had friends hiding out for the big moment! I was one closet door away from ruining the whole surprise!

I really didn't think he'd be able to surprise me since I knew he had the ring, but because of the last-minute decision to move early, I didn't see it coming at all.

Which leaves us where we are today. Renovating the beautiful home I bought in Oklahoma, with the adorable pup we just adopted, Maki. It feels like the start of the rest of our lives, and it is.

Epilogue

The Bachelor not only led me to the love of my life, but it also became a journey of self-discovery and empowerment for me.

Even though I believed I had fully integrated my disability into my identity post-college, the passing of my beloved Granny revealed a hidden truth: I was still holding back. Her absence sparked a desire within me to step beyond my comfort zone and to embrace life wholeheartedly, including all aspects of my disability.

Entering the world of reality television, I was confronted with challenges and opportunities that I couldn't believe were possible. I never thought I could be on national television and deal with all the ups and downs that came with that. Never thought I'd have a platform to speak about hearing loss and cochlear implants. But now, I can't imagine life any other way.

Who would I be if I hadn't chosen this path? I don't know.

The same way I'll never know who I would be without hearing loss, and I don't want to. Because like my mom always said, everyone has a place in the world, and I think this was always meant to be mine.

I'm still young, with more growing to do, and a lot of life to live. But if there's anything I can hope for in the future, it's that I can aim to reach others facing similar struggles, whether it's navigating between communities or reconciling disability with personal identity. Maybe there's someone out there like high-school Abigail, unsure of where she fits in if she isn't capital-D deaf but also isn't hearing.

Or maybe there's someone like my mom, who is going through the hearing loss journey as a parent. Or someone like Noah who wants to be as supportive as possible to their partner with hearing loss. Or anyone with a disability who doesn't know where to draw the line between that disability and who they are as a person. It's a role I never anticipated, but one I've come to cherish deeply.

Reflecting on my journey, I've come to understand the importance of embracing all facets of my identity. For too long, I resisted being labeled as "the deaf girl" fearing it would overshadow my individuality as Abigail. But by doing this, I cost myself so much. I hid any part of me that felt connected to my disability. It didn't matter if accommodations would've helped me succeed, I shunned them, because that meant embracing my hearing loss. And to me, embracing hearing loss was embracing the identity I didn't want to have.

Even during my time on *The Bachelor*, I grappled with how the audience perceived me. While I aimed to educate and raise aware-ness throughout the experience, I often felt reduced to a single aspect of my identity. It was a struggle to reconcile the desire to share my story with the risk of being typecast. I became "the deaf contestant" and along with that title it seemed like people viewed me as fragile, not noticing the qualities beyond my dis-ability. While I wanted to share my experiences with a cochlear implant, it wasn't easy to feel like the deaf girl again.

Yet, through the support of my loved ones and being able to connect with so many others on a similar path, I've learned how to embrace every part of who I am. I love sharing my disabil-ity with the world, but I also know I'm more than my disability. Now, as I interact with viewers through social media and share my story in this book, I attempt to break down stereotypes and inspire others to embrace their true selves. I've come to realize that authenticity is my greatest strength, and by owning my iden-tity, I can empower others to do the same.

So, even though I may always carry the label of "the deaf girl," I've come to realize that I am more than that. I am Abigail—a woman of strength and with a voice of resilience and courage. This realization didn't happen overnight, nor was it perfect, but what's important is it has brought me to where I am today.

Through these pages, I hope to empower others to embrace their truth, to stand tall in the face of adversity, and to live boldly and unapologetically in who they are.

Just as I have learned to do.

Acknowledgments

As I reflect on the creation of *The Deaf Girl*, I am filled with gratitude for the individuals who played a pivotal role in bringing this memoir to life.

At the core of my appreciation is my family.

My mom, Suzie, a guiding force throughout the process, not only lent her unwavering support but actively contributed to the shaping of this story. She, at a younger age than I find myself now, navigated the uncharted waters of having two daughters under the age of two, both with hearing loss. My mom's sacrifices during those early years were monumental, and her support has left a mark on the person I am today. In writing our shared journey in this memoir, I aspired to do justice to the resilience and love she poured into us. I owe my confidence, strength and the ability to share this story to the foundation she laid during those formative years.

My sister, Rachel, who shared this extraordinary journey with me. She paved the way, becoming my other half and perpetually remaining my biggest fan. This memoir is not only a reflection of my experiences but also a celebration of the bond we share, the challenges we've overcome, and the unspoken language that connects us.

My dad, Weston, who wasn't deterred or intimidated when he met my mom who had two young daughters with hearing loss. Instead, he stepped in, becoming a pivotal force in our cochlear implant journey. His unwavering support and active involvement in this journey showed me the greatest example of unconditional love and acceptance.

My younger brothers, Alistair and Stuart, who have always been pillars of support. Even in moments that may have been difficult, such as watching their older sister date on TV, their understanding and encouragement has always been present.

My Granny and Grandpa, Marie and Arthur, whose sacrifices and steadfast commitment became the cornerstone of our journey. When my mom found herself alone with two daughters, they immediately took us under their wing. Their positivity, presence at countless appointments, and dedication to practicing speech therapy with us elevated them into more than grandparents; they became our second set of parents. My Granny, now a cherished memory, played an integral role in my story. I sincerely hope that the voice captured within these pages echo the pride she instilled in me. To my grandpa, whose love endured even when faced with the reality of his granddaughter appearing on *The Bachelor*, it's been the biggest blessing to be your granddaughter. It is my hope that this book serves as a testament to the pride and love both my grandparents have showered upon me.

My Grandma and Grampa, Nancy and Weston, thank you for being such big supporters. Your love, encouragement, and excitement for my life updates has been something I'll always treasure.

To Noah, my fiancé and biggest supporter. Your love has been a constant, embracing me for who I am and encouraging me to share my story. During moments of doubt, particularly when I questioned whether anyone would read this book, he stood by me, urging me to continue. His encouragement played a role in shaping this memoir, and I can't express enough gratitude for his belief in the importance of our story.

To all my friends over the years, even those I may not talk to now, I extend a huge heartfelt thank you. Your influence has played a significant role in shaping who I am today. I appreciate your acceptance and the fact that I was never defined by my disability in your presence. Growing up, I felt included and supported, and I owe a part of that to each of you.

To Lori, my exceptional manager, thank you for being a driving force behind the scenes and for helping me share my story with the world.

To Haylee, my gifted ghostwriter, for transforming my experiences into a vivid and compelling narrative. Her ability to grasp and articulate my deepest emotions has been truly remarkable.

Thank you for bringing my story to life in ways I couldn't have envisioned.

To Courtney at LGR Literacy, whose belief in my story made sharing it with the world possible. Your support and positivity throughout the process not only facilitated the project but also made me believe in its potential.

Thank you to the team at Sourcebooks for turning my vision into a reality: my editor, Kate Roddy; Kayleigh George, Sr. Director of Marketing; Liz Keslch, Director of Marketing; Sarah Brody, Associate Art Director; and Emily Proano, Senior Production Editor.

And finally, to all of you, I extend my deepest appreciation for your support. Sharing my journey with you over these past few years has been a true pleasure. Whether you're personally affected or supporting a loved one with hearing loss, my deepest hope is that you found solace, understanding, and perhaps a bit of inspiration within these pages. Thank you for allowing me to be a part of your lives.

About the Author

Abigail Heringer, a prominent deaf advocate, speaker, and social media influencer, emerged into the public eye after captivating audiences on ABC's *The Bachelor*. Born profoundly deaf, she embraced the transformative potential of a cochlear implant at the age of two and embarked on her journey of navigating the intricacies of a hearing world.

After her appearance on *The Bachelor*, Abigail continued her advocacy for the deaf community. She uses her platform to shed light on the triumphs and challenges of living with a cochlear implant with her followers. Abigail has a degree in finance from Linfield University.

Abigail is currently engaged to her fiancé Noah, whom she met on *Bachelor in Paradise*. They reside in Tulsa, Oklahoma, accompanied by their German shepherd, Maki.